About This Book

Why is this topic important?

Although the use of technology for training is on the rise, live, in-person instructor-led train-ing is still the most common way in which training is delivered. In many organizations, people with little or no experience in the field are asked to deliver training workshops. Those people need easily accessible information and practical tools that help them prepare for and deliver successful workshops.

What can you achieve with this book?

In today's rapidly changing organizations, people need to be able to do more with fewer re-sources. Those who are new to training do not have the luxury of time in which to learn how to deliver training workshops that meet individual needs and the organization's goals. This book is an easy-to-use resource that provides practical information, best practices, proven strategies, tips, and tools for delivering training workshops that achieve results.

How is this book organized?

Chapters 1 through 5 cover the process of planning and preparing for a workshop. Trainers learn how to schedule training, notify participants, prepare materials and supplies, and pre-pare themselves to conduct the workshop. Chapters 6 through 10 provide information and strategies for delivering training, including how to handle nervousness, open and close and a workshop, manage the group, help people learn, and evaluate the success of training. Each chapter includes questions, worksheets, and application activities to enhance learning. At the back of the book is a list of resources.

About Pfeiffer

Pfeiffer serves the professional development and hands-on resource needs of training and human resource practitioners and gives them products to do their jobs better. We deliver proven ideas and solutions from experts in HR development and HR management, and we offer effective and customizable tools to improve workplace performance. From novice to seasoned professional, Pfeiffer is the source you can trust to make yourself and your organization more successful.

Essential Knowledge   Pfeiffer produces insightful, practical, and comprehensive materials on topics that matter the most to training and HR professionals. Our Essential Knowledge resources translate the expertise of seasoned professionals into practical, how-to guidance on critical workplace issues and problems. These resources are supported by case studies, worksheets, and job aids and are frequently supplemented with CD-ROMs, websites, and other means of making the content easier to read, understand, and use.

Essential Tools   Pfeiffer's Essential Tools resources save time and expense by offering proven, ready-to-use materials—including exercises, activities, games, instruments, and assessments—for use during a training or team-learning event. These resources are frequently offered in looseleaf or CD-ROM format to facilitate copying and customization of the material.

Pfeiffer also recognizes the remarkable power of new technologies in expanding the reach and effectiveness of training. While e-hype has often created whizbang solutions in search of a problem, we are dedicated to bringing convenience and enhancements to proven training solutions. All our e-tools comply with rigorous functionality standards. The most appropriate technology wrapped around essential content yields the perfect solution for today's on-the-go trainers and human resource professionals.

Pfeiffer
www.pfeiffer.com

Essential resources for training and HR professionals

Delivering Training Workshops

Pfeiffer Essential Guides to Training Basics

Janis Fisher Chan

Pfeiffer
A Wiley Imprint
www.pfeiffer.com

Library of Congress Cataloging-in-Publication Data

Chan, Janis Fisher.
    Delivering training workshops / Janis Fisher Chan.
        p.   cm. — (Pfeiffer essential guides to training basics)
    Includes bibliographical references and index.
    ISBN 978-0-470-40467-6 (pbk.)
        1. Employees—Training of.   2. Employee training personnel.   3. Training.   4. Workshops (Adult education)   I. Title.
    HF5549.5.T7C5337 2010
    658.3'124—dc22

                                                                    2009031949

Acquiring Editor: Matthew Davis
Director of Development: Kathleen Dolan Davies
Production Editor: Dawn Kilgore

Editor: Rebecca Taff
Editorial Assistant: Lindsay Morton
Manufacturing Supervisor: Becky Morgan

Printing   10 9 8 7 6 5 4 3 2 1

Contents

Introduction

I was in graduate school the first time that I ever taught a course. It was a one-week summer session class on dramatic literature, and the professor who was scheduled to teach it had become seriously ill a few days before. "You know the material," she told me from her sickbed when I protested that I didn't know how to teach. "Use my notes. You'll do fine."

But although I studied my professor's notes carefully, I was a wreck when it came time to stand up in front of the students, most of whom were teachers who were taking the class for the extra credits they needed to keep their jobs. On the first day, my hands shook and my mouth was so dry that I could hardly get out the words, "Good morning." I stumbled through that first meeting, hardly looking up from my notes, trying to ignore upraised hands so I didn't have to answer questions. By the time the three-hour session was over, I was exhausted.

The next day was a little easier. Once I managed to lift my eyes from my lecture notes, I found a few friendly faces with interested expressions and discovered that making eye contact with people actually helped me relax. A question that one of the students asked triggered a discussion that seemed to energize everyone. A couple of students stopped on their way out to say, "Thanks."

Each day went better than the one before. I discovered how much easier and more effective the class was when I engaged the students in the learning process instead of lecturing at them for three hours. By the end of the week, I had learned at least as much about teaching as the students had learned about dramatic literature. I didn't know it at the time, but that experience would form the foundation of a lifelong career that has been focused on one primary goal—helping people learn.

About the Pfeiffer Essential Guides to Training Basics

The three books in this series, *Training Fundamentals, Designing and Developing Training Programs,* and *Delivering Training Workshops,* provide practical ideas,

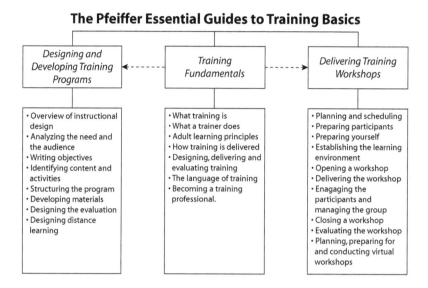

The Pfeiffer Essential Guides to Training Basics

Designing and Developing Training Programs	Training Fundamentals	Delivering Training Workshops
• Overview of instructional design • Analyzing the need and the audience • Writing objectives • Identifying content and activities • Structuring the program • Developing materials • Designing the evaluation • Designing distance learning	• What training is • What a trainer does • Adult learning principles • How training is delivered • Designing, delivering and evaluating training • The language of training • Becoming a training professional.	• Planning and scheduling • Preparing participants • Preparing yourself • Establishing the learning environment • Opening a workshop • Delivering the workshop • Enagaging the participants and managing the group • Closing a workshop • Evaluating the workshop • Planning, preparing for and conducting virtual workshops

information, tips, and techniques for people who are new to the training field as well as trainers who have been in the field for a while and would like to learn more.

Training Fundamentals

This book is a no-nonsense, practical overview of training. Here's what you'll learn:

- What training is and the role it plays in helping organizations achieve their goals
- What a trainer does and the characteristics and skills a trainer needs to be successful
- The ways in which training is delivered
- The adult learning principles that guide successful training programs
- What's involved in designing training to meet specific needs, delivering a training workshop, and evaluating training success
- The terminology and acronyms commonly used in the training field
- How you can develop yourself as a training professional

Designing and Developing Training Programs

Building on the basics provided in *Training Fundamentals*, this book guides you through the instructional design process, providing practical ideas, information, tools, and strategies you can use immediately. You'll learn how to:

- Make sure that training is needed, relevant, and cost-effective
- Analyze the needs and characteristics of the audience
- Write the behavioral learning objectives that form the foundation of a training program
- Decide what content to include
- Select activities that engage people and help them learn
- Organize content and activities into a workable structure
- Develop trainer's guides, participant workbooks, slide presentations, and other learning materials
- Design a program evaluation
- Design virtual and remote training programs

Delivering Training Workshops

Also building on the basics of delivery presented in *Training Fundamentals*, this book provides strategies, best practices, tips, and guidelines you can use immediately to prepare for, deliver, and follow up on a workshop. You'll learn how to:

- Plan and schedule a workshop
- Prepare participants so they know what to expect and arrive ready to learn
- Increase your confidence by preparing yourself to conduct training
- Establish an environment that is conducive to learning
- Get started in a way that immediately engages participants
- Present information clearly, keep people involved, and respond to questions
- Manage the group and keep the workshop on track
- Close a workshop in a way that helps participants use what they learn
- Evaluate the success of a workshop
- Plan, prepare for, and conduct virtual workshops

How to Use This Book

This book expands on and adds to the concepts and ideas presented in *Training Fundamentals*, so if you have read that book, you will find some of the information familiar. The focus in that book, however, was to provide an overview of the process of delivering training workshops, while this book provides greater detail and practical techniques for putting the process to use.

Like the other two books in the series, this book is designed as a learning tool. You'll find questions and suggested activities that will help you think about what you are learning, make connections between new learning and what you already know, and apply what you learn. The answers to the questions are either apparent in the text or appear at the end of the chapter. I encourage you to answer the questions and do the activities, but feel free to skip any that don't seem relevant. In other words, this is your book; use it the way that works best for you.

Check What You Know
When you see this icon, you'll find questions that help you see what you already know about the topic or subtopic.

* *

THINK ABOUT IT

When you see this icon, you'll find questions that help you think about something that you have learned.

* *

Quick Quiz

From time to time, you'll find a quiz that will help you check your understanding of the material.

Apply What You Learn

When you see this icon, you'll find questions or an activity to help you apply the learning to a real situation.

Before You Begin

One theme that you'll find throughout the *Training Basics* series is the importance of helping people apply what they learn in training to real-world situations. That's the purpose of the activities that close most of the chapters—to help you apply the learning to a training project of your own. Choose a project that you can think about as you read this book and describe it on the next page. The project should be a training workshop that you need to deliver. If you have no real, current project to work on, think of a workshop that you might provide for people at your company or for people at another organization, such as a nonprofit or community group.

Briefly describe the topic of your workshop:

_____

_____

Who is the audience for this workshop?

_____

_____

Why is this training program needed? What is it intended to accomplish?

_____

_____

_____

_____

Your Objectives

Another important theme that you will find in each book of the series is that it's easier to get somewhere when you know where you are going. Think about what you would like to accomplish by reading this book and briefly describe your objectives below:

_____

_____

_____

_____

_____

_____

_____

_____

_____

_____

Enjoy learning!

1

Preparing for a Workshop

Check What You Know

In her position as a new trainer for 21st Century Software, Cybelle has been asked to deliver a workshop on meeting planning for team leaders. She's pleased to have been given this responsibility. She's also excited, and a little nervous. Although she has facilitated many meetings, she has never delivered a training workshop. Seeking advice, she calls Leon, a colleague from her last job who has been delivering training workshops for more than twenty-five years.

"I'll be glad to help," Leon says. "What would you like to know?"

"Everything!" Cybelle says. "I don't even know where to start."

"Well, let's start there," Leon laughs. "The first thing you need to do is prepare for this workshop. I've got a little free time tomorrow. We can go over the essential tasks and some of the things to keep in mind while you do them."

What are some of the tasks that Leon might tell Cybelle that she needed to do to prepare for her workshop? What are some of the things that he might suggest she keep in mind?

_____

_____

_____

_____

_____

_____

When you go to the theater, the production you see didn't spring into being a few minutes before the curtain went up. It is the result of weeks, even months, of careful preparation to ensure that all the elements—the lighting, the sets, the sound, the costumes, the actors—work together seamlessly to provide a unique theatrical experience, to set a mood, to make you laugh, or cry, or wonder, or think. Successful workshops also do not just happen—the foundation for success is laid long before the participants walk into the room. It takes careful preparation for all the elements to work together to provide participants with a seamless learning experience.

Here's what you'll find in this chapter:

- The importance of preparation to the success of a workshop
- What's involved in preparing for a workshop
- What to consider when preparing for a workshop

Much of the difference between success and failure has to do with one simple word: preparation.

Karen Lawson, *The Trainer's Handbook* (2nd ed.)

1. The Importance of Preparation

Check What You Know

Which of the statements about preparing for a workshop are accurate?

1. _____ Nervousness at the beginning of a workshop can result from insufficient preparation.
2. _____ Experienced trainers rarely neglect to prepare adequately for a workshop.
3. _____ Trainers sometimes think of preparation as something that takes them away from their real work.
4. _____ Trainers who neglect the preparation process might never succeed at setting up an environment that is conducive to learning.

Even trainers who fully understand the importance of preparation may neglect to give it enough time and attention. They go about the process in a haphazard way, squeezing preparation tasks into an already overcrowded schedule. They make room requests, and send out notices to participants, and then forget to follow up. They don't get around to preparing handouts or looking at the script until the last minute. They lie awake the night before the workshop, anxious about whether things will work out okay, and then rush into the room a few minutes ahead of the participants, only to find that the setup is wrong, equipment is malfunctioning, or essential materials and supplies are missing. When participants start to arrive, they are busy rearranging furniture, unpacking boxes, or fumbling with the slide projector. They get started late and then feel surprisingly nervous, their mouths dry and their voices tremulous as they try to find their places in the script while participants roll their eyes and wonder what kind of day they're in for.

That kind of start to a workshop can be very hard to overcome. Trainers who neglect the preparation process risk appearing less professional and credible, often find it difficult to establish rapport with participants, and may never succeed at setting up an environment that is conducive to learning.

People who are new to training may neglect to prepare properly because they don't realize what's involved and what the results of inadequate preparation are likely to be. But even experienced trainers sometimes neglect certain aspects of preparation. Preparing for a workshop takes time, often more time than trainers expect, and trainers sometimes consider preparation time as something that takes them away from their "real" work. They forget that preparing to conduct a workshop *is* an important part of their real work. Preparation time is also an investment: when it's used thoughtfully and carefully, it pays big dividends in the form of a workshop that runs smoothly and achieves results.

2. What's Involved in Preparation

Like any project, the process of preparing for a workshop involves lots of tasks. You might be responsible for carrying out all of those tasks yourself, or you might have help with some of them, such as those related to making the logistical arrangements, notifying participants, and preparing the materials. But even if you do not carry out all the tasks yourself, keep in mind that you have a real stake in whether or not everything is done, and done right, because you are the one who will have to deal with any problems on workshop day. And, as you will see, there are certain preparation tasks that only you can do.

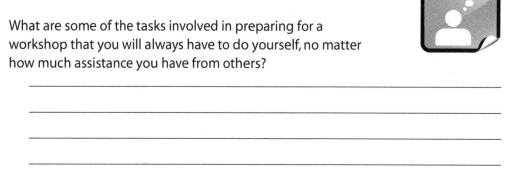

THINK ABOUT IT

What are some of the tasks involved in preparing for a workshop that you will always have to do yourself, no matter how much assistance you have from others?

_____

_____

_____

_____

The tasks involved in preparing for a workshop fall into several general categories. You'll learn about them in detail in the following chapters. First, here's an overview:

- *Scheduling the workshop and planning the learning environment.* Scheduling can be one of the most challenging tasks in the preparation process. You can't have a workshop without participants, but finding times when everyone who wants or needs to attend is available can be a logistical nightmare. You need a physical environment that is conducive to learning, but learners' schedules need to be coordinated with facility availability. Your workshop might require the participation of subject-matter experts, company executives, outside speakers, or others, whose schedules also need to be considered. Finding dates when everyone and everything you need are available can take some time, so it's very important to start this process as early as possible.

- *Selecting and notifying participants.* People are selected for training in different ways. Some are self-selecting—they make the decision to attend a workshop on their own, because they are interested in the topic or think that the training will be useful to them. Some have no choice about attending—the training is required for their work. Others are "strongly encouraged" to attend by their managers or others, possibly to improve a real or assumed performance deficiency or to prepare them to take on new responsibilities. Some will already be familiar with the workshop because they were involved in its design; many will learn about the training for the first time when they receive notice that they have been enrolled. From a trainer's perspective, the way in which participants are selected and the way in which they learn about the workshop can have significant effects on their readiness to learn.

Producing and obtaining materials and supplies. It's easy to spot a trainer in an elevator—she's the one with rolled-up flip-chart pages under her arm and a laptop over her shoulder, dragging a huge suitcase behind her. Workshops require lots of stuff—trainer guides, handouts or participant workbooks, prepared flip-chart pages, posters, name tents, writing tables, marking pens, props, videos, game materials, and more. All that stuff takes time to produce and assemble. To avoid last-minute panic and keep from exhausting yourself before the workshop, think carefully about exactly what you need and leave enough time to produce or obtain each item. Otherwise, you might have to spend the day before the workshop running around looking for props and putting workbooks together—and still discover that you're missing something important when the session begins.

Preparing participants for training. People who walk into a workshop knowing only the title, the location, and the time are likely to spend most of the first hour or so trying to figure out what it's all about and what it has to do with them. On the other hand, those who have a good understanding of why the workshop is being held, what will be covered, how the subject relates to them and their work, and the ways in which the training will benefit them are more likely to arrive ready to learn. The more you can do to prepare participants for the workshop, the more quickly you will be able to engage them in the learning process.

Preparing yourself to conduct training. When I was in my first two years of college, I would often spend most of the night before a big test trying to catch up with all the studying I'd neglected during the semester, drinking cup after cup of coffee and forcing myself to stay awake as long as I could. The next morning, I'd drag myself bleary-eyed into the classroom for the

> ## What's Involved in Preparation
>
> - Scheduling the workshop and planning the learning environment
> - Selecting and notifying participants
> - Producing and obtaining materials and supplies
> - Preparing participants for training
> - Preparing yourself to conduct training
> - Making contingency plans

test. It wasn't until I was in my senior year that I finally learned there was a better way—that if I prepared for tests and papers ahead of time, I'd do better, because I'd arrive relaxed, rested, and far more clear-headed.

Preparing yourself is one of only a few workshop preparation tasks that you must do yourself. But it's not only one of the most important tasks, it's one that many trainers leave until the night before the workshop, when they should be relaxing and getting some rest. The time you spend getting to know the workshop inside and out and practicing your delivery pays big benefits. The more prepared you are, the more credible you will seem, the more confidence you will project, the less nervousness you'll experience, and the more smoothly the workshop is likely to go.

Making contingency plans. It's a fact of life that, no matter how carefully you plan and prepare, something is likely to go wrong. There is so much involved in putting on a workshop that you can expect at least a few problems—misunderstandings about the room setup, malfunctioning equipment, missing supplies, people being called out to deal with emergencies. Of course, you can't anticipate everything, but thinking ahead of time about what could go wrong and preparing backup plans will keep you from feeling anxious and make it easier to deal with problems so that they do not derail the workshop.

3. What to Consider When Preparing for a Workshop

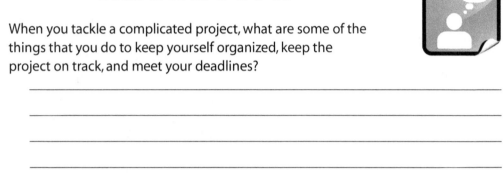

THINK ABOUT IT

When you tackle a complicated project, what are some of the things that you do to keep yourself organized, keep the project on track, and meet your deadlines?

_____

_____

_____

_____

Preparing for a workshop is like carrying out any other project: the more organized you are, and the more attention you pay to the details, the better the chances of achieving your goals. Here are some suggestions for using the preparation process to best advantage so that both you and your learners are ready on workshop day.

- *Use checklists.* Detailed checklists that include responsibilities and deadlines help you stay organized, ensure that you don't miss anything, and let you spot problems early enough to resolve them easily. Like to-do lists, your checklists should be reviewed and updated at least once a day—more often if necessary. See the sample checklist on page 9 for some ideas.

- *Confirm and reconfirm all the logistical arrangements.* There are few things worse than arriving at the training site to find that the facilities people have lost the room reservation, although a close second is having the room set up entirely wrong and finding that none of the equipment or material you need is there. No matter who makes arrangements for the facility, the setup, the equipment, the materials, and the refreshments, confirm every little detail yourself. Then confirm them again so that you will not arrive on the day of the workshop to find that the slide projector is missing and no one ever saw the room setup instructions—or that the room has been given away to someone else.

- *Learn as much as you can about the participants.* Why are people attending this training? How much do they already know about what to expect? What jobs do they do? Do they work closely together or are they strangers? Will managers and their direct reports be attending the workshop together? The more you know about the participants, the more easily you'll be able to adapt the content and activities to meet their specific needs and the more prepared you'll be for issues that might come up during training.

- *Make contact with participants before the workshop.* Even if someone else signed people up, get in touch with participants in person, by phone, or by e-mail to introduce yourself, explain the reasons for the workshop, provide a preview, and describe what to expect during the session. If it's appropriate, give participants a brief pre-workshop assignment that helps them start thinking about the topic—and perhaps prepares them for an opening activity. Making a personal connection with the participants ahead of time will make it easier to establish rapport and help both you and them feel comfortable on workshop day; providing them with key information about the workshop and stimulating their thinking about the topic helps prepare them to learn.

Sample Preparation Checklist

Workshop Title: _____

Workshop Date: _____

Task	Responsibility	Complete by	Confirm by
1.			
2.			
3.			
4.			
5.			
6.			
7.			
8.			
9.			
10.			

To Consider When Preparing for a Workshop

- Confirm and reconfirm all the logistical arrangement.
- Learn as much as you can about the participants.
- Make contact with participants before the workshop.

Quick Quiz

List the three to five key learning points from this chapter that will be most helpful to you.

_____

_____

_____

_____

_____

Apply What You Learn

Use the Preparation Checklist at the end of the chapter to help you prepare for your next workshop.

What's Next?

Now that you have an overview of what needs to be done to prepare for a workshop, you're ready to examine each of the important tasks in more depth. In the next chapter, you'll learn how to handle the complicated task of scheduling a workshop and plan an environment that will be conducive to learning.

Answers to Exercise

Check What You Know

Which of the statements about preparing for a workshop are accurate?

1. _X_ Nervousness at the beginning of a workshop can result from insufficient preparation.
2. ___ Experienced trainers rarely neglect to prepare adequately for a workshop.
3. _X_ Trainers sometimes think of preparation as something that takes them away from their real work.
4. _X_ Trainers who neglect the preparation process might never succeed at setting up an environment that is conducive to learning.

Preparation Checklist

Make a preliminary checklist of tasks that need to be done to prepare for your workshop. Indicate whether you or someone else will do each task. Include dates by which a task needs to be done and dates on which you will confirm arrangements.

Workshop Title: _____

Workshop Date: _____

Task	Responsibility	Complete by	Confirm by
1.			
2.			
3.			
4.			
5.			
6.			
7.			
8.			

2

Scheduling the Workshop and Planning the Learning Environment

Check What You Know

Leon has helped Cybelle make a preliminary checklist of the tasks that she needs to complete to prepare for the meeting planning workshop. "Both the timing of the training and the training environment can affect people's ability to learn," he told her. "So you need to get started right away to schedule the workshop and plan the learning environment."

"Can't I just pick the date and go from there?" Cybelle asked.

"It's usually more complicated than that," Leon said. "Here's why."

What do you think Leon might have told Cybelle to keep in mind when she schedules the training and makes decisions about the learning environment?

_____

_____

_____

_____

_____

_____

When my brother and I decided to throw a 50th wedding anniversary party for our parents, we chose a date, sent out "hold the date" notes to our family members and our parents' friends, and then went looking for a place to hold the party. We had a few criteria: the location needed to be near our parents' home, it needed to be large enough for about sixty people, and it needed to be within our budget. Needless to say, we also wanted it to be beautiful and comfortable.

But finding the right place proved difficult. It turned out that there was a big event scheduled in the area for the same weekend—not only were there no facilities that met our criteria available, but all the hotels where our guests might stay were fully booked. We had no choice but to change the date.

We sent out another note with a new date and started looking again. We had just found the perfect site when we learned that my mother's favorite sister wouldn't be able to come on the date we'd chosen. She suggested another date, but the caterer we wanted to use wasn't available on that date.

That kind of juggling went on for a couple of weeks: the facility, the guests, the caterers—we couldn't seem to coordinate the various schedules. Finally, just as we were about to settle for a facility that was less than perfect or a caterer we were unsure about, everything fell into place. We ended up holding the party in a beautiful winery, the food was great, everyone except two cousins no one really knew was there, and it was a wonderful celebration. But the story does exemplify the challenges involved in scheduling, especially when it involves lots of people and a limited number of desirable sites.

In this chapter you'll learn about:

- Why scheduling a workshop can be tricky
- What to consider when scheduling
- How to avoid common scheduling pitfalls
- How to choose a training room
- How to set up the environment in a way that helps people learn

1. What to Consider When Scheduling

THINK ABOUT IT

Suppose you need to schedule a workshop for twenty-five managers who will be delivering performance evaluations in six weeks. What are some of the factors you would need to consider when selecting dates for the workshop?

_____

_____

_____

_____

You may not be responsible for selecting the date or dates for every workshop that you deliver—in fact, some workshops will already have been scheduled by the time you come on the scene. But sooner or later those tasks are likely to fall to you. Because scheduling can become so complicated, it's important to learn what's involved, how to make the process go as smoothly as possible, and how to avoid common scheduling pitfalls.

Some of the important factors to consider are how soon training needs to be held; when both participants and facilities are available; what times of year and days of the week should be avoided; whether there is something going on that could distract participants' attention; and how long it will take to prepare and obtain essential materials and supplies. If the workshop requires guest speakers, subject-matter experts, or special equipment, you will also need to find out when those people and things will be available.

Let's look more closely at each of those factors.

When Do Participants Need to Be Trained?

Many training programs are time-sensitive, meaning that training needs to be delivered by a certain time. Loan officers may need to get up to speed on new regulations before those regulations take effect in a few weeks. Managers may need to know how to prepare end-of-year reports before the end of the fiscal year. Supervisors may need to enforce safety regulations as soon as possible to reduce accidents. Staff members who are about to be posted to an overseas facility may need an understanding of the culture in which they will be working before they start to pack.

Even when there is no actual date by which training needs to be held, there might be other reasons for scheduling it as quickly as possible. Perhaps the company's reputation and bottom line are being affected by product defects, valuable employees are jumping ship because they don't like working with their managers, or an increasing number of clients are complaining about poor service.

Check What You Know

Which of the following statements are generally accurate when it comes to scheduling a workshop?

1. _____ Fridays are usually good days for training because people appreciate an early break from work.
2. _____ The first two weeks of December can be good times for training in some organizations because not too much else is going on.
3. _____ The first two weeks of January are nearly always a terrible time for training because people's attention is still on the holidays.
4. _____ Four-day weeks are often good for training because there are fewer meetings in those weeks.
5. _____ June, July, and August can be good months in which to schedule training because people are more relaxed in the summer.

When Are Participants Available?

As mentioned earlier, it can be difficult to find dates that work for everyone. It's easier, of course, when all the participants are part of an intact team, work at the same location, work the same shifts, and seldom travel; even then, you still need to schedule around vacations, busy times, and deadlines. And scheduling can turn into a logistical nightmare when participants are drawn from different areas of the organization, work in vastly separated locations, and travel often.

The reality is that it is sometimes impossible to find a date that works for everyone who wants or is expected to attend a particular workshop. Here are some strategies you can try:

- *Hold more than one session*. If there are enough participants to offer multiple sessions of the same workshop, you might be able to offer a choice of dates. Each of the sessions might have fewer participants, but as long as you have the minimum number of people needed for a successful workshop, that's not necessarily a disadvantage. For one thing, small groups are easier to manage.

- *Hold sessions in different locations*. If workshop participants are widely disbursed and you are able to offer multiple sessions, consider holding sessions in different locations. It's easier for participants to fit workshops into busy schedules when they don't have to travel; it's also usually much less expensive to bring a trainer to the participants than the other way around.

About Group Size

Like so many things about training, there are no hard-and-fast rules about group size. But there are a few guidelines:

- For participants to be able to engage in activities that involve discussion and collaboration, the minimum group size is about six to eight people.
- Groups with more than twenty to twenty-five participants can become unwieldy—fewer people are able to participate during discussions, and managing the group can be more challenging.
- When large groups are unavoidable, it's important to break people into smaller groups for activities, and you might need to involve co-trainers to help monitor groups and give people feedback as they work.

Think about times to avoid. There are certain times when it is more likely that participants will be able to focus their attention on training. For example, in some organizations, the week after Thanksgiving and the first two weeks of December can be good for training because not too much else is going on. I've also found that January can be a good time for training—the year is just getting started and people might not be too heavily immersed in new projects. Although it's hard to say what times are best for a specific organization and group of participants, here are some times that I've found are usually good to avoid:

- *Busy seasons*. Every business has its busy season—tax time and end of the fiscal year for accountants, late fall for people in retail sales— during which people are likely to be unusually busy, distracted, or unavailable.

- *Big events*. People are likely to be unavailable or distracted during the weeks leading up to and immediately following a big event, such as an important product launch or an annual conference.

- *Mondays and Fridays*. In general, it's a good idea to avoid scheduling training on the first and last days of the workweek, when people are coming back from or thinking about their weekends, taking a day off, trying to plan their weeks, or trying to finish things before the weekend.

- *Weeks with a holiday*. Weeks in which a holiday shortens the workweek to four days are seldom good for training because some people take those weeks off, and those who do not might be trying to squeeze five days of work into four or covering for colleagues who are on vacation. In particular, it's best to avoid weeks with major holidays such as Thanksgiving or the Fourth of July.

- *Weeks with children's school vacations*. The summer months, the spring school break, and the last two weeks of December are almost always bad times for training. People with families naturally tend to schedule vacations when kids are out of school.

Be Aware of Cultural and Religious Holidays

When you are scheduling training, check to see whether the dates you are considering fall on cultural or religious holidays that any of the participants might observe, such as the Asian New Year, Yom Kippur, or Ramadan. Also, many countries observe holidays that are not observed in the United States, so if you are scheduling training in another country, find out what local holidays you need to consider.

Using Calendar-Sharing Technology When Scheduling Training

Teams are increasingly using calendar-sharing technology that allows people to coordinate their schedules for meetings, appointments, and events. Having access to workshop participants' calendars can simplify the scheduling process; it can also help you make sure that participants have blocked off the time.

Check What You Know

Why is it important to think about what training rooms are available when scheduling training? What role does the room play in the success of a workshop?

_____

_____

_____

_____

When Is the Right Room Available?

You might have no choice about where to hold training—your organization has only one training room, and it's scheduled on a first-come, first-served basis. But under most circumstances, you'll need to make two key decisions before scheduling a room. The first is whether to hold the workshop on site ("in house") in one of the organization's conference or training rooms, or in an off-site facility such as a hotel or conference center. The next is which room to choose from the choices that are available on the date or dates that you're considering.

It can be more than worthwhile to change the date of a workshop in order to get the right room. I've conducted training in noisy lunchrooms, cavernous lecture halls, conference rooms that were like fishbowls with picture windows onto a hallway, cramped classrooms with fixed chairs squashed together like coach seats on an airplane. I can tell you from experience that it's an uphill battle to overcome the deficiencies of the wrong room.

In fact, finding the right room is so important that you might want to reserve the room or ask the facilities manager to hold some dates even before you know exactly when the participants will be available—it's much easier to change a room reservation than to rearrange a lot of individual schedules. It's the chicken-and-the-egg thing: Which comes first? In the end, you might have to go back and forth between participants' availability and room availability until you find the right dates. (There's more on what to look for in a training room later in this chapter.)

How Much Time Will It Take to Produce or Obtain Workshop Materials?

You can easily photocopy a few handouts the day before a workshop. But most workshops have more complicated materials requirements: slides, printed workbooks, computer software, posters, props, videos, assessments, materials for games, and more.

Be realistic when estimating how much time it will take to produce or obtain everything you'll need—things often take longer than you think they will. Leave plenty of time in the schedule so that you won't have to rush around at the last minute finishing the slide presentation, assembling workbooks, or finding game materials. Make a checklist that shows what you need, who's responsible for producing or obtaining each item, and a deadline by which each item will be ready. (There's more about preparing materials and supplies, along with a sample checklist, in Chapter 4.) Leave a little extra time for everything, just in case there are delays.

When you are estimating how long it will take to get everything ready, consider the following:

- *Other people's priorities.* If other people are responsible for providing any of the materials, remember that your workshop is probably not among their top priorities. Find out how much time they will need, make sure that they know your deadlines, and ask them to let you know right away if they run into problems. Check in from time to time to see how they are progressing and whether they need anything from you. If someone doesn't seem to be getting around to an important task, the person may be too busy with other things; in that case, consider finding someone else to do it.

- *The type of materials.* It can take quite a while to produce certain kinds of materials, such as software, simulations, videos, or complicated games. Make sure that you know how long it will take to produce those materials before scheduling the workshop.

- *The location of the workshop.* If materials will need to be shipped to the training site, schedule them to arrive at least two or three days early, and make a backup plan, in case the shipment doesn't show up.

When Are Guest Speakers, Subject-Matter Experts, and Others Available?

People other than you and the participants might need to be there for all or part of the workshop. Does the CEO plan to make an introduction? Does the human resources manager need to be around to answer questions? Do members of a product development team need to provide a demonstration? Is a consultant coming in to conduct an experiential activity? If other people are important to the success of the workshop, you'll need to find out when they will be available and consider their schedules with those of the participants and the facility. In fact, finding out when key people are available might even be the first step in the scheduling process.

When Is the Equipment Available?

In most organizations, there is a limited supply of projectors, TV monitors, flip-chart easels, video cameras, and other equipment, so when you reserve the room, also check to make sure that what you need to run the workshop will be available. If your workshop requires anything special, such as the prototype for a new product or equipment for a demonstration, find out when it will be ready before settling on the workshop dates.

To Consider When Scheduling Training

- When do participants need to be trained?
- When are participants available?
- When is the right room available?
- How much time will it take to produce or obtain workshop materials?
- When are guest speakers, subject-matter experts, and others available?
- When is the necessary equipment available?

Scheduling Virtual Workshops

Scheduling a virtual workshop—one that will be held in an online meeting room, instead of in a physical training room—can be as challenging as scheduling a live, in-person workshop. You need to find out when the online meeting room and the technical people who manage it are available and match their availability with that of the participants. If participants are located in widely disbursed time zones, you'll have to juggle times of day as well as dates.

2. Planning the Learning Environment

Check What You Know

For a workshop on team problem solving, which of the seating configurations on the next few pages would be most likely to help people learn? why?

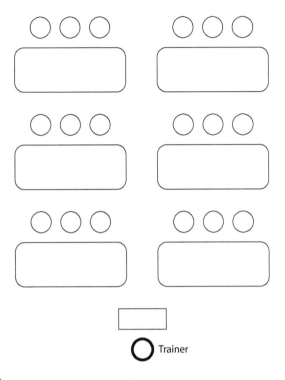

Trainer

Room Setup A

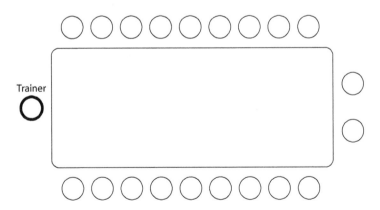

Trainer

Room Setup B

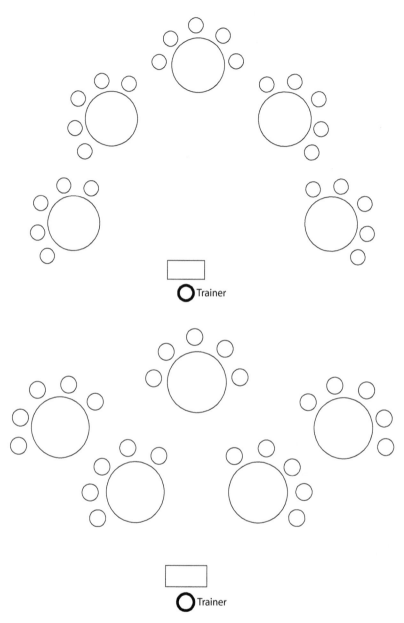

Trainer

Trainer

Room Setup C

THINK ABOUT IT

Think about some workshops that you've attended. In which rooms were you the most comfortable? Which rooms provided an environment in which you found it easiest to learn? Based on your experience, what characteristics should a trainer look for in a training room?

_____

_____

_____

_____

_____

A friend of mine used to give parties that that didn't quite work. There never seemed to be a comfortable place to sit or stand, and getting to the food table was always a trial. It was odd—when there were only a few people there, her home was comfortable and pleasant to be in. But when she set up for the party she somehow transformed the room from a relaxed, inviting space into an uncomfortable, stuffy, boxed-in space in which it was awkward to move and difficult to hold a conversation. She set up all the straight-backed dining chairs around the perimeter, forcing everyone into the center. She pushed the dining table into the corner, which meant that only two or three people could get to it at one time, and then they had to push back through the crowd balancing their plates and wine glasses. She also kept the windows closed, so as the night went on, the room would be stuffier and stuffier.

Just as the physical environment made my friend's parties less enjoyable, the physical environment of a workshop can have a significant impact on how well people are able to learn. It's hard to concentrate if the training room is too small and crowded, too noisy, too hot or cold; if the chairs are uncomfortable; if you have to crane your neck to see other people when they're speaking; or if other people in and out during discussions.

Selecting the Training Room

There are some characteristics that all good training rooms have in common: they are the right size, well-lit, not too warm or too cold, well-ventilated, and accessible to all participants. Other characteristics you'll need in a room depend on what people will be doing in the workshop—Working in small groups? Discussing confidential or sensitive issues? Using computers? Doing activities that require moving around? Working on their own? Using equipment?

Think about how large and flexible a space you'll need. Consider the need for privacy. Try to visualize the participants interacting with you and one another, watching demonstrations, doing the activities. Imagine the ideal room—and then try to get as close to it as you can.

If there are no suitable rooms on site, find out whether there's enough money in the budget to rent a room at a hotel, a conference center, or a community college. Check out the room in person if you can—a hotel facility manager's idea of an acceptable training room may differ significantly from yours. If the facility is too far away for you to see the room in person, ask lots of questions to be sure that it will meet your requirements. For example, you can request a layout that shows the size and shape of the room, as well as the location of the windows. Ask about the lighting and the ventilation system. Discuss the kinds of chairs and tables that will be available. Also, make sure that the facility can provide the equipment you will need, such as projectors, DVD players, TV monitors, and flip-chart easels, and reserve that equipment when you reserve the room.

At a minimum, the training room should meet these requirements:

- *Size and shape.* The room should be large enough so that participants can be seated comfortably at tables, but not so large that they feel dwarfed in the space. In general, square rooms are easier to set up than long, rectangular rooms. A room that is too large will be easier to transform into a learning environment in which people can feel comfortable and interact easily than a room that is too small, in which people are likely to feel cramped.

- *Flexibility.* Fixed seating, such as a single large conference table—or worse, auditorium-style seats and immovable podiums—limits interaction and can make it very difficult to do activities. Do everything in your power to avoid those kinds of setups. Instead, try for as much flexibility as possible so that you can set up the room the way you want it and rearrange the seating if necessary for specific activities. (There's more on room setups below.)

- *Good light and air.* Stuffy, dimly lit rooms make it hard for people to stay awake and pay attention. The room should be well-lit, but not so bright that people feel the need to put on their sunglasses, with a ventilation system that keeps the air circulating. If there are windows—which I always prefer—there should be curtains or blinds that can be closed if there is too much sunlight.

To Change the Size and Shape of a Room

You can't do much about a room that's too small except to make the best of it. But you can alter the feel and functionality of a room that's too large and rectangular. To create a "square" room of the right size, arrange the seating at one end, instead of scattering the tables all over the room, and use screens to close off the unused part of the space.

- *Privacy.* People are uncomfortable learning when they are on display to others. Make sure that the room has a door that closes and curtains or blinds for any windows that offer a view of the interior from public spaces such as hallways and courtyards.

- *Wall space for posting flip-chart pages.* In most workshops, you'll want to post flip-chart pages that you've prepared in advance and some of those on which you record information that you will refer to later. For example, you might post the agenda, participants' ideas and strategies, key learning points from activities, and a "parking lot" for issues that come up during the workshop.

- *Free from noise and other distractions.* Loud music on the other side of a room divider, jackhammers outside the window, people wandering in and out— all those things make it hard for people to concentrate during a workshop. You can't control everything, of course, but try to find a room that's as quiet and free from distractions as possible so people can concentrate on learning.

- *Easy access to restrooms and food.* It uses up time when people have to go onto another floor or into another building to attend to their personal needs and find something to eat; it can also be hard to get people back once they leave the immediate area. If you have a choice of rooms, choose one that's not too far away from the restrooms. Unless you're providing refreshments (recommended), try to choose a room that's relatively close to the cafeteria or vending machines.

- *A convenient location.* A pretty little conference center with a training room that looks out over a lovely garden might be an appealing place in which to hold training. But if it's too far out of the way, getting there might be difficult for the participants. If you're holding training off site, make sure that it is in a convenient location. Think about how long it will take people to get there, whether there is enough parking, and whether the site is accessible by bus or train for people who do not drive. If participants will have to travel for more than their normal commute time, consider starting the workshop a little later than you would if it were on site.

- *Accessible to participants with special needs.* Every participant, including those who have difficulty walking or have other special needs, should be able to access the training room easily. That means finding a room that people can reach without walking up stairs or wandering through miles of corridors. Consider access to the building as well as access to the room. It doesn't help to have an elevator inside the building if there is a long flight of stairs from the sidewalk or the street.

There's a Facility Checklist at the end of the chapter.

Breakout Rooms

Your workshop might include activities that require breakout rooms—areas other than the training room in which participants can work. For example, you might need breakout rooms if small groups need privacy to collaborate on a project or to practice for a presentation.

Breakout rooms do not have to be large. Participants might be able to work in a corner of a lounge or at a table in a cafeteria (except at lunch hour). Breakout groups might need easels and flip-chart pads to use for brainstorming or to record key points from their discussions.

Choose breakout rooms or areas that are in close proximity to the training room so that you can circulate among the groups to monitor their work and offer support if they need it—and so you can quickly get people back into the training room when the time for the activity is up. Try not to let people use their offices as breakout rooms—there will be too many distractions.

Delivering Training Workshops: Pfeiffer Essential Guides to Training Basics.
Copyright © 2010 by John Wiley & Sons, Inc.
Reproduced by permission of Pfeiffer, an Imprint of Wiley. www.Pfeiffer.com

In-House or Off-Site?

There are advantages and disadvantages to holding a workshop at the workplace or off-site, at a hotel, conference center, or college.

Using an on-site training room is less expensive, and it's usually more convenient for most if not all of the participants. You may have more control over the way the room is set up, and you won't have to haul or ship boxes of materials to the training site. Participants might be more comfortable in a familiar space.

On the other hand, participants are easily distracted when the workshop room is close to where they work. They may be tempted to go back to their desks during breaks, only to get caught up in a "crisis." Their colleagues might come in and interrupt the workshop with questions that they think cannot wait.

In an off-site training room, which is more private and free from the immediate distractions of the workplace, participants can usually focus more easily on learning. But off-site training rooms can be expensive, the setup is harder to control, and you will have to ship—or carry—all the materials to the facility. The facility location might not be convenient for all the participants, and those who feel uncomfortable not being directly connected with what's going on at work are likely to duck out every time their cell phone or BlackBerry vibrates.

Delivering Training Workshops: Pfeiffer Essential Guides to Training Basics.
Copyright © 2010 by John Wiley & Sons, Inc.
Reproduced by permission of Pfeiffer, an Imprint of Wiley. www.Pfeiffer.com

Doing Training at a Hotel

Holding a workshop in a hotel conference or banquet room has a few special challenges. Those rooms are usually designed more for events such as parties, weddings, and meetings than for workshops, so it's very important to be specific about your needs. Discuss the arrangements in detail with the facility manager—in person, if possible. Provide a detailed diagram of the setup you want. Ask whether the hotel has all the equipment you need, including flip-chart easels, a screen, and cables to hook up your laptop to the projector so you'll know whether there is anything you'll need to bring yourself. Explain that you need stable tables that will not shake or collapse when people are working. Pay special attention to the size of the room—many hotel meeting rooms are too small for a workshop, while others are the size of a ballroom. Check out the lighting. Some hotel conference rooms have bright, florescent lights that can be very annoying, while others use "mood" lighting that is too dim for a workshop. Consider bringing in standing lamps to soften lighting that is too bright or add lighting to an overly dim room.

Check What You Know

Which statements about planning the room setup are accurate?

1. _____ The way the room is set up sends a message about whether the focus of the workshop is on the trainer or on the learners.
2. _____ Classroom-style seating, where all the participants face the trainer, is often preferable because it makes it easier to keep order in the training room.

(Continued)

3. _____ A podium can create a barrier between the trainer and the learning group.
4. _____ A setup in which people sit at round tables with four or five people at a table encourages participants to interact.
5. _____ Conference-style seating, with all the participants seated around a fixed rectangular or oval table, makes it easy for people to see and hear one another, no matter how large the group.

Planning the Room Setup

The way the room is set up affects more than whether participants can see and hear easily. The room setup can have a significant impact on people's ability to learn.

There are several key decisions to make when planning the room setup, including how the seating will be arranged; where to place flip-chart easels, the projector and screen, and other equipment; where you will stand to address participants; where you will put your trainer's notes or script, materials, and supplies; and where you or the caterer will put refreshments.

Participant Seating

The seating arrangement affects the tone of the workshop, the ways in which the participants interact with you and with one another, and the dynamics of the group. Certain arrangements send the message that this is an informal, learner-centered workshop; others convey the message that this is a formal classroom environment, with the focus on the trainer. Some arrangements make it easy for people to interact with one another, some limit interaction. Some encourage active participation, some do not.

There are some seating arrangements that I try to avoid because I do not find them useful for training. One is the traditional formal classroom setup, with the trainer in front of the group and the participants seated at rectangular tables arranged in parallel rows facing front. That setup makes it hard for people to see and work with one another, and it makes the trainer seem to be the most important person in the room. People in the back of the room may have trouble hearing people in the front when they speak, and they might be less likely to speak up themselves. They might also have trouble seeing the trainer and the flip charts.

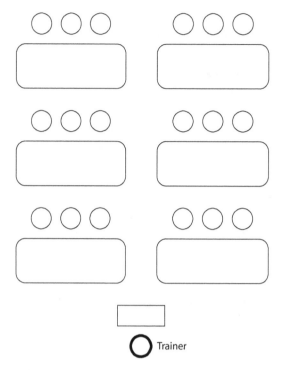

Traditional Formal Classroom Style

Auditorium Style

Even worse than classroom style, however, is auditorium seating, where participants sit in fixed chairs, sometimes with little spring-up writing desks.

That setup puts the focus squarely on the trainer, makes people uncomfortable, discourages interaction, and makes most activities nearly impossible.

Another configuration I try to avoid is the conference table setup, with participants and trainer seated at one large table; unless the group is very small, that setup not only makes interactive activities difficult, but people cannot easily see those who are on the same side of the table.

Conference table seating has an advantage over traditional classroom style because people can see and hear one another more easily. But this setup feels to most people more like a meeting than a learning event. It makes it difficult for participants to work on activities either individually or in small groups, and it's hard to get them up and moving around. If the table is too large, people are too far away from one another; if it's too small, they'll be crowded together. People may find it hard to see and hear those who are seated on the same side as themselves, especially if the table is rectangular instead of oval.

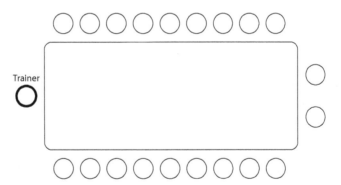

Conference Table Seating

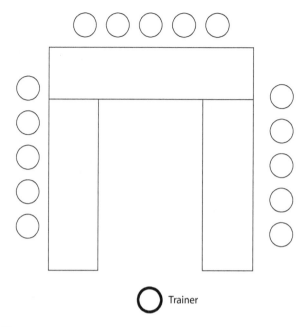

Trainer

Conference–U

A variation of fixed conference table seating is what I call the "conference-U," one or more rectangular tables across the back of the room, with two "legs," forming a U-shape with open space inside the U.

Although this setup is more flexible than a single conference table, I find it somewhat formal, and it has some of the same issues: for example, people cannot easily see the people along the same side of the table as themselves.

Because engagement and interaction are so important to the learning process, I prefer a seating arrangement that makes it easy for people to see, hear, and talk with one another; gives them enough room to work in small groups and on their own; and conveys a message that the focus of the workshop is on the learner, not the trainer.

The setup I like best has round tables that are large enough for four or five people to sit comfortably, with enough space between the tables so that group discussions do not intrude on one another and I can walk easily around the room to observe and give feedback while people work.

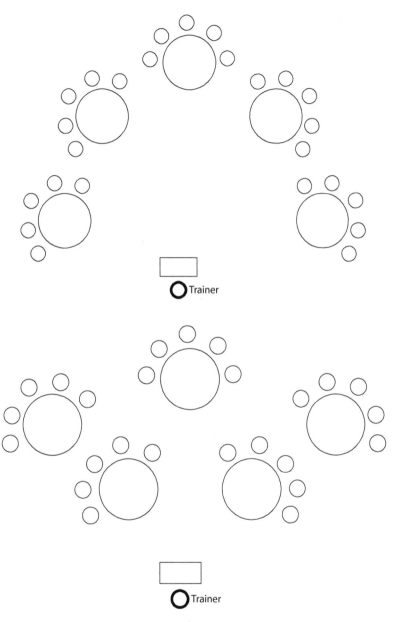

Trainer

Trainer

Round Tables

When only rectangular tables are available, I usually set them up in a chevron shape, also with sufficient space between them.

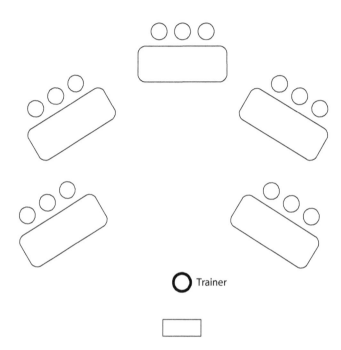

Rectangular Tables in Chevron Shape

Trainer Presentation Area

When you address the participants, they need to be able to see you easily, and you need to be able to make eye contact with them. A speaker's podium that fixes you firmly in one place creates a barrier between you and the group. But you need somewhere to put your notes and script, so a good alternative is to use a small table placed to the side or at the front of the presentation area, leaving a clear space in which you can move freely as you talk and listen to the participants.

Equipment

Anyone who has been a trainer for any length of time has tripped over electric cords, gotten bruises from bumping into the metal cart that holds the slide projector, or knocked over unstable flip-chart easels. Try to have the room set up in a way that places equipment so that it is as unobtrusive as possible and you can move around without bumping into things. Ask that electric cords be taped down and request the smallest table possible for the projector. If you're using a television monitor to show DVDs, make sure it can be pushed to the side when not in use. Place the flip-chart easels where everyone in the room can see them and they do not block the screen. Check the stability of the easels before participants arrive and try to get replacements for any that seem likely to collapse.

> ## Check Tables for Stability
>
> Remember how annoying it is when your table at a restaurant wobbles when you cut your food? Wobbly, unstable tables can also be annoying in a workshop, and things that are annoying can distract people from the learning process. If facilities has provided round tables, make sure that the tops are securely fastened to the bases; if the tables are the fold-up rectangular kind, make sure that the legs are fully locked and the tables sit firmly on those legs. Check the tables before participants arrive and do what you can to have broken or unstable tables replaced.

Supplies and Refreshments

Tables for supplies and refreshments should be placed where they are accessible but where they will not get in the way or draw attention during presentations and activities—the back or the side of the room is usually best.

Food and Drink

When people visit your home, it's polite to offer something to eat and drink. Offering refreshments in the morning when participants arrive and at mid-morning and afternoon breaks helps people feel welcome and makes them more comfortable. It also makes it less likely that they will disappear to the cafeteria or down the street to a café during breaks.

Refreshments don't have to be expensive—coffee, tea, water, and a box of Trader Joe's cookies will do. But if your budget allows, a Continental breakfast encourages participants to arrive early and mingle before the workshop begins. And everyone appreciates having bottled water, juice, sodas, and snacks available in the afternoon.

If you use an in-house service or outside caterer for refreshments, be sure to place the order well in advance, specify the exact time that you want the refreshments delivered, and confirm the arrangements shortly before the workshop. If you are providing lunch, choose food that is not too heavy—lasagna and garlic bread with chocolate cake for dessert might taste great, but that meal might put people to sleep in the early afternoon. Also, make sure to remember when planning the menu that the group might include vegetarians or people with dietary restrictions.

Quick Quiz

List the three to five key learning points from this chapter that will be most helpful to you.

_____

_____

_____

_____

_____

What's Next?

Workshops are more likely to be successful when the participants arrive ready to learn. You'll discover what you can do to help them get ready in the next chapter.

Apply What You Learn

Use the worksheet at the end of the chapter to schedule and plan the learning environment for your next workshop.

Answers to Exercises

Check What You Know

Which of the following statements are generally accurate when it comes to scheduling a workshop?

1. ___ Fridays are usually good days for training because people appreciate an early break from work.
2. _X_ The first two weeks of December can be good times for training in some organizations because not too much else is going on.
3. ___ The first two weeks of January are nearly always a terrible time for training because people's attention is still on the holidays.
4. ___ Four-day weeks are often good for training because there are fewer meetings in those weeks.
5. ___ June, July, and August can be good months in which to schedule training because people are more relaxed in the summer.

Check What You Know

For a workshop on team problem solving, which of the following seating configurations would be most likely to help people learn? Why?

Room Setup C

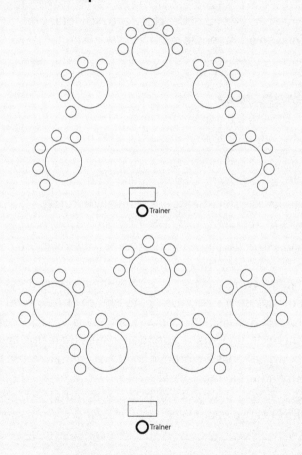

This seating configuration encourages interaction and makes it easier for people to work on activities in small groups, a key component of the learning process.

Check What You Know

Which statements about planning the room setup are accurate?

1. _X_ The way the room is set up sends a message about whether the focus of the workshop is on the trainer or on the learners.
2. ___ Classroom-style seating, where all the participants face the trainer, is often preferable because it makes it easier to keep order in the training room.
3. _X_ A podium can create a barrier between the trainer and the learning group.
4. _X_ A setup in which people sit at round tables with four or five people at a table encourages participants to interact.
5. ___ Conference-style seating, with all the participants seated around a fixed rectangular or oval table, makes it easy for people to see and hear one another, no matter how large the group.

Delivering Training Workshops: Pfeiffer Essential Guides to Training Basics.
Copyright © 2010 by John Wiley & Sons, Inc.
Reproduced by permission of Pfeiffer, an Imprint of Wiley. www.Pfeiffer.com

Facility Checklist

☐ Size and shape appropriate for the size of the group and the nature of the workshop.

Notes: _____

_____

☐ Flexible seating arrangements.

Notes: _____

_____

☐ Good light and air.

Notes: _____

_____

☐ Temperature controllable.

Notes: _____

_____

☐ Sufficiently private.

Notes: _____

_____

☐ Enough wall space for posting flip-chart pages.

Notes: _____

_____

Delivering Training Workshops: Pfeiffer Essential Guides to Training Basics.
Copyright © 2010 by John Wiley & Sons, Inc.
Reproduced by permission of Pfeiffer, an Imprint of Wiley. www.Pfeiffer.com

☐ Free from noise and other distractions.

   Notes: _____

   _____

☐ Easy access to restrooms.

   Notes: _____

   _____

☐ Easy access to food and drink.

   Notes: _____

   _____

☐ Convenient location.

   Notes: _____

   _____

☐ Accessible to participants with special needs.

   Notes: _____

   _____

Plan the Learning Environment

Use this worksheet to schedule your workshop and plan the learning environment.

When do participants need to be trained?

By this date: _____

Within this period: _____

☐ No particular timetable

List any dates/days of the week/times of day that need to be avoided because of participants' prior commitments and work schedules, conflicting events, or organizational priorities, holidays, or other circumstances.

_____

_____

What dates/days of the week/times of day would be best?

_____

_____

List the guest speakers, subject-matter experts, and others who need to be there for all or part of the workshop and indicate whether there are any dates/days of the week/times of day that they cannot be available.

_____

_____

List any dates on which the room you want to use or the equipment you need is not available.

_____

_____

How long will it take to produce or obtain workshop materials?

_____

_____

Sketch a room setup for your workshop. Include the seating configuration, the presenter area, and the placement of refreshment and supply tables.

3

Preparing Participants to Learn

Check What You Know

Leon asked Cybelle, "How will participants be selected for your meeting planning workshop?"

"I don't know," Cybelle admitted. "Don't people usually just sign up?"

"Sometimes they do," Leon explained. "But in some cases, the first time they find out about the training is when they get a message saying that their manager has signed them up. You'll want to find out how people were selected for training and why they'll be attending the workshop."

Leon went on: "You also need to think about how you're going to prepare them for training. The more prepared they are when they walk in the door," he said, "the easier it will be to engage them in the material. Besides," he added, "you might be able to save some time during the workshop by giving them some pre-work."

"Pre-work?" Cybelle asked. "You mean like homework, only before the workshop?"

Leon laughed. "I guess you could call it that."

"You said I needed to prepare people for training. How can I do that?"

"Let me give you some suggestions," Leon said.

(Continued)

What are some of the suggestions that Leon might have made to help Cybelle prepare the team leaders for the meeting planning workshop?

_____

_____

_____

_____

I used to teach business writing workshops for a university business extension program. Those workshops were challenging in a number of ways. One challenge was that I had no idea about why people had signed up and no opportunity to interact with them before they arrived on the first day. Luckily, most people were taking the workshop because they had a real need to improve their business writing skills, and those people usually came fully prepared to learn. But others were there because they had been "strongly encouraged" by their managers to take the workshop. Those people sometimes wandered in with a look on their faces that said, "My body is here, but don't expect *me* to be here."

I eventually learned how to connect with reluctant participants, although there were a few whose evaluations indicated that they would rather have scrubbed floors than come to my workshop. But my job would have been much easier if I'd been able to give people a preview of what they were going to learn, help them see how the learning would be useful to them, and get them thinking about the topic of business writing even before they walked into the room.

Here's what's covered in this chapter:

- How participants are selected and notified about training

- Using pre-work assignments to engage participants and prepare them for training

- Gaining the support of participants' managers

1. How Participants Are Selected

Check What You Know

1. What are some of the reasons that people attend a training workshop?

   _____

   _____

   _____

2. Why is it important for trainers to know why people are attending their workshops?

   _____

   _____

   _____

   _____

As trainers, we like to think that people come to a workshop because they are passionately interested in the subject and want to learn as much as they can about it. But in the real world, people come to training for many different reasons. Some have a choice, some do not. Some see training as an opportunity, some see it as punishment. Some recognize the long-term value of learning, others see training as taking valuable time away from more important tasks. An understanding of why people are attending gives you some insight into what they need to know before they arrive and what you can do to prepare them so that they get the most out of the workshop.

For a given workshop, people might be selected in a number of different ways: the participants themselves may have requested the training and been intimately involved in the planning process; people might have signed up because they saw the workshop description in a catalogue or received an e-mail announcement and thought it might be useful to them; for some, the training might be a job requirement or part of a performance improvement or development process; a few people take every workshop they can, either because they like to learn or because they see training as a way to get away from work for a few hours.

You often have little involvement in the selection process and little control over the ways in which participants are selected, although you might be able to establish prerequisites or guidelines to limit participants in a particular workshop to those with specific knowledge, skills, or characteristics. When you are not involved in the selection process, however, it's important to find out why people are attending. For example, if the training is mandatory or participants were signed up by their managers, you might need to make a special effort to make sure that they understand how the training will be useful to them.

Marketing Your Workshop

Sometimes trainers are responsible for drumming up interest to encourage people to sign up for a workshop. When that's the case, try these strategies:

- Design a flier with interesting, relevant graphics that will catch people's attention and post the fliers in public places around the organization— lunchrooms, bulletin boards, employee lounges. Briefly describe the four or five most important things that people will learn in the workshop, focusing on what the participants are likely to find the most interesting and important. Include the date, time, and place, and the URL of a website and/or an e-mail address and a phone number so people can learn more.
- Send an e-mail announcement to everyone who might be interested in this workshop. Like a flier, the announcement should be brief, interesting, and well-designed, providing just enough information to capture people's interest and letting them know how to find out more information.
- Get in touch with managers whose employees might benefit from this training. Explain the purpose and how the training will be useful to the employees, the manager, and the organization. Give the managers a list of talking points or a sample e-mail message to make it easier for them to inform their employees about the workshop.
- Hold "brown-bag" lunches for people who might be interested in the subject. Deliver a mini-workshop, hand out fliers, and answer questions.

Delivering Training Workshops: Pfeiffer Essential Guides to Training Basics.
Copyright © 2010 by John Wiley & Sons, Inc.
Reproduced by permission of Pfeiffer, an Imprint of Wiley. www.Pfeiffer.com

The success of your presentation is 50 percent assured if your audience's interest is working for you from the beginning.

Bob Pike, *Creative Training Techniques*

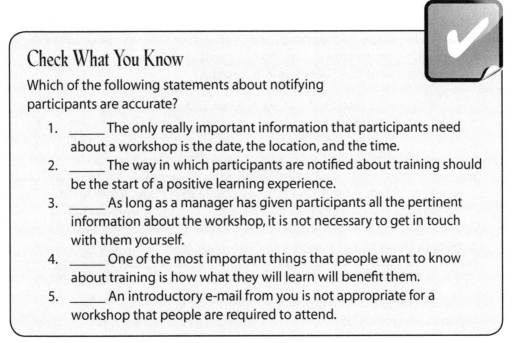

Check What You Know

Which of the following statements about notifying participants are accurate?

1. _____ The only really important information that participants need about a workshop is the date, the location, and the time.
2. _____ The way in which participants are notified about training should be the start of a positive learning experience.
3. _____ As long as a manager has given participants all the pertinent information about the workshop, it is not necessary to get in touch with them yourself.
4. _____ One of the most important things that people want to know about training is how what they will learn will benefit them.
5. _____ An introductory e-mail from you is not appropriate for a workshop that people are required to attend.

How Participants Are Notified

Just as participants are selected in different ways, there are different ways in which they learn about what to expect from the training. Even those people who sign up on their own may have selected the workshop on the basis of the title alone, without knowing much about the content, the objectives, or what kind of training experience to expect. If their manager or the HR director has enrolled them, they might know only that they are supposed to appear at a certain time and place to attend a workshop on the subject of XYZ.

But the process of notifying participants about a workshop should be more than telling them the title and giving them the logistical detail. It should be the beginning of a positive learning experience. Before they arrive at the training room, participants need a clear understanding of why the workshop is being held; what content will be covered; and, most importantly, how what they learn will benefit them. They should also have started thinking about the topic, especially how it relates to their own experience and what they already know.

Even if participants were notified about the workshop by someone else, it's important to make a personal contact with them yourself. Your initial contact, which can be in person, by telephone, or in an e-mail message, should set the friendly, positive, professional tone that you will carry into the workshop. Here's an overview of the information to provide:

- *The workshop title, date, location, and time.* Include the logistical details, even if you think that participants already have them, and encourage them to put the workshop on their calendars. Include the full title of the workshop; the day (or dates), including the day of the week; the exact location; and the starting and stopping times. For full-day workshops, say whether lunch is being provided. If the workshop is being held off-site, provide detailed directions, including a printed map or a link to a map, transportation options, parking instructions, and the telephone number of a contact person at the facility. If people will need to travel to reach the workshop site, tell them how to make travel and lodging arrangements and suggest that they arrive far enough ahead of time so that they do not feel rushed.

- *A brief description of the workshop and the reasons it is being held.* Describe the workshop and the purpose in a statement of three sentences or less that will capture the participants' attention and stimulate their interest, such as: "The results of the recent company-wide assessment indicate that more than 65 percent of the employees think that they spend too much time in unnecessary or unproductive meetings. This workshop will provide team leaders with practical information and techniques they can use immediately to plan and conduct meetings that make the best use of everyone's time and help us achieve our business goals."

- *How the workshop will benefit them.* Whether training is required for their jobs or they have signed up for a workshop because they are interested in the topic, adult learners want to know why they are learning—how what they learn will be useful to them. A brief statement or short list of benefits can spark their interest and help them begin to relate to what they are going to learn. For example: "As a team leader, you want to make the best use of your and your team members' time so you can achieve your goals. The techniques you learn in this workshop will help you . . . ." (There is a sample of a workshop invitation e-mail on page 54.)

What's in It for Me (WIIFM)

When we were kids, we went to school because that's what we were expected to do: learning was our job. But by the time we finished twelve or sixteen or eighteen years of education, we had become much more selective. As adults, we want to know *why* we are using our time to learn something when we could be doing something else.

Experts in adult learning do not agree on everything, but they do agree that people learn best when they have a clear understanding of how the learning will benefit them in their real world—how it will make their jobs easier, improve their performance and their productivity, or help them to advance in their careers. A key question that adult learners ask is, "What's in it for me?" As training guru Bob Pike says in *Creative Training Techniques*, "Every person in your audience is going to be tuned in to radio station WII-FM."

The learning objectives and the agenda. The learning objectives provide details about what the workshop will help people accomplish, and the agenda gives them a preview of the workshop content. If your initial contact is by e-mail, you can include the objectives and agenda as an attachment. When sending out the agenda, however, it's a good idea to leave off specific times (except for the starting and stopping times), because the timing is always subject to change.

What Participants Need to Know

- The logistics—the workshop title, date, location, and time
- A brief description of the workshop and why it is being held
- How the workshop will benefit them
- The learning objectives and the agenda

Delivering Training Workshops: Pfeiffer Essential Guides to Training Basics.
Copyright © 2010 by John Wiley & Sons, Inc.
Reproduced by permission of Pfeiffer, an Imprint of Wiley. www.Pfeiffer.com

Sample "Welcome" e-Mail to Workshop Participants

Dear Melinda,

I am glad that you will be attending the Managing Your Priorities workshop that I am conducting on March 6 in the Bayside Training Room (Building C, Second Floor). We'll have a Continental breakfast ready by 8:45 and the workshop will start promptly at 9:00. We'll be done by 5:00.

This workshop will provide practical ideas and techniques that will help you use your time more productively so you can achieve your goals. You'll learn a system for determining what's important; how to plan and schedule your time; how to anticipate and deal with problems; and more. (See the attachment for the learning objectives and the agenda.)

So that we can use the workshop time as efficiently as possible, there are two things that I need you to do:

1. Complete the attached questionnaire and return it to me by February 25. Your responses will help me make sure that the workshop meets your needs. I will not share them with anyone.
2. Make a list of everything that you need to accomplish during the four weeks from March 6 to April 6. Include the things you need to do in your personal life as well as at work. Bring the list to the workshop.

There's a place on the questionnaire for questions you have about this workshop. If you would like to ask your questions directly, please feel free to get in touch with me at the telephone number or e-mail address below. I look forward to seeing you at the workshop.

Best wishes,

Sending Reminders

People are often so busy that they tend to forget things, even those that are clearly marked on a calendar. (That's why doctors' offices and hairdressers routinely make calls to remind people about their appointments.) It's a good idea to send reminders to participants—and perhaps, to their managers—a few days before the workshop. Include the logistics—date, time, and place—in case they've mislaid the original information. Remind them of what they need to bring and, if necessary, what they are supposed to do before the workshop. Include another copy of the agenda and stress the importance of arriving on time. Ask people to let you know right away if something has come up that would make them come late or prevent them from attending.

2. Using Pre-Work Assignments to Engage and Prepare Participants

Check What You Know

Which of the following would be useful pre-work assignments for a workshop on being a better manager?

1. _____ Ask participants to read the book on which the training program is based and come prepared to discuss it in the workshop.
2. _____ Ask participants to think of the best manager they have ever known, list the characteristics that made that person a good manager, and bring the list to the workshop.
3. _____ Ask participants to complete an assessment of their own management strengths and challenges.
4. _____ Ask participants to prepare a biographical report about a successful manager.

People are busier than ever these days in both their personal and professional lives. Participants are likely to arrive at your workshop with a lot of things on their minds—a report that needs to be written, a problem that needs to be solved, a budget that needs to be prepared, a teacher-child conference that needs to be scheduled. It can be very challenging to help them shift focus from their day-to-day issues to learning. That's one of the functions of pre-work: to engage people in the learning process and get them thinking about the topic before they arrive in the training room.

Pre-work assignments take many forms: something to read, a set of questions to answer, some information to collect, even a puzzle to figure out. These assignments need not—in fact, they should not—be lengthy. But they do need to be relevant to the subject of the workshop and interesting enough to capture the learners' attention.

Examples of pre-work assignments include:

- Questions that stimulate participants' thinking about their expectations for the workshop and what they want to accomplish, such as: "What are your objectives for this workshop? What would you like to know more about and be able to do more proficiently when the workshop is over?" or "What would you like the trainer to cover during this workshop? What questions do you have about [the subject]? What issues would you like the trainer to address?"

- Questions that stimulate participants' thinking about the subject, such as: "Think about your best and worst experiences as a customer. Describe what happened" or "In this workshop, you will learn how to be a coach. Take a few minutes before the workshop to think about what coaches do."

- A brief written or video case study or scenario that participants will discuss in the workshop: "This case presents a situation in which a manager is dealing with a performance problem. So that we can use valuable workshop time efficiently, please take a few minutes to read [or view] the case before the workshop and be prepared to discuss it."

- A self-assessment: "During this workshop, you will use the results of the attached questionnaire to evaluate your leadership strengths and challenges. Please complete the questionnaire and return it by March 6. You will receive a summary of the results during the workshop."

- A research project in which participants gather information that they will use in the workshop: "Please take a few minutes to find three examples of . . . and be prepared to share them with your colleagues during the workshop."

- Samples of work they have done before the workshop or information for a project they can work on during the workshop: "Please send three samples that you think are representative of your writing" or "Please bring information for a business plan you are working on."

The Pre-Work Challenge

Even though pre-work can be an excellent way to help prepare participants for training, it can be a challenge to get everyone to do it. Here are some suggestions:

- *Explain why the pre-work is important and how it will be used.* Describe the purpose of the assignment and explain the way in which it will be used during the workshop.

- *Make sure that pre-work is relevant.* Depending on the group, it might be fine to send something that's fun to do, like a crossword puzzle or a scavenger hunt,

Delivering Training Workshops: Pfeiffer Essential Guides to Training Basics.
Copyright © 2010 by John Wiley & Sons, Inc.
Reproduced by permission of Pfeiffer, an Imprint of Wiley. www.Pfeiffer.com

but fun is not enough. The assignment should not take too long to do and the relationship between the pre-work and the topic of the training program should be clear: "This crossword puzzle will help you find out how much you already know about the terminology that patient schedulers commonly use. Give it a try—we'll go through the answers during the workshop."

Keep pre-work assignments brief and tell people approximately how long they will take to complete. It's best to limit pre-work to something that people can do in less than thirty minutes—fifteen or twenty minutes is even better. Asking people to read books or lengthy articles or assigning a complicated research project are exercises in futility. Few people will actually complete the assignment, making it useless either as a way to prepare participants to learn or as the basis for workshop activities.

Make it easy for people to do the pre-work. For example, when asking people to answer questions, provide a template or form for their responses, or use an online questionnaire. When asking them to read something, send it as a PDF file or include a link to the website on which they will find it. If you want them to view a video clip, give them a direct link so they can get to it quickly.

Ask for people to send you something, and give them a deadline. People are more likely to do the pre-work if they have to submit something by a specific date: "Please return the completed questionnaire by May 5 so I can tally the responses" or "Please complete the online assessment by May 5 so I can print out your report in time for the workshop." Follow up if people have not responded by the deadline.

Tips for Using Pre-Work

- Explain the purpose of the pre-work and how it will be used.
- Keep pre-work relevant.
- Keep pre-work assignments brief.
- Provide a template or form, preferably online.
- Send the necessary documents or links.
- Ask people to respond in some way.

Preparing Participants for a Virtual Workshop

It's just as important to prepare people for a virtual workshop as for a live, in-person workshop. Most of what you've learned about notifying and preparing participants applies to virtual workshops, although there are a few differences. Here are some points to keep in mind:

- *Consider the technical requirements.* Make sure that all the participants have the necessary technology and equipment to be able to attend and participate in the virtual workshop. At a minimum, they will need a computer with a fast Internet connection and a telephone, preferably with a headset; they might also need a microphone. The people who manage the virtual training room should be able to supply you with the requirements and help you make sure that people will be able to connect on workshop day.

* *Make a personal contact ahead of time.* It can be more difficult to engage people in a virtual workshop because you do not have the advantage of the face-to-face interaction that is so important for establishing rapport, especially at the beginning of a workshop. Thus, it is even more important to make a personal contact by phone and/or e-mail with participants ahead of time so you can introduce yourself, stimulate their interest in the workshop, and help them see what's in it for them.

* *Use pre-work to get people involved.* Just as in a live, in-person workshop, pre-work is a great way to get people involved in the learning process before the virtual workshop begins. Make sure the pre-work meets all the criteria discussed earlier in this chapter.

* *Tell people what to expect.* Some participants are likely to be unfamiliar with the virtual workshop format, or to expect a virtual workshop to be a presentation that they simply watch and listen to. Explain how the process works, pointing out that this will be an interactive workshop in which they will be answering polling questions, asking questions of their own, doing activities, and perhaps working with other participants in breakout rooms. If possible, consider providing participants with an introduction to the use of the virtual workshop tools before the training. Encourage them to get in touch with you before the workshop if they have questions about the process.

* *Send handouts and other materials ahead of time.* A few days ahead of time, send out any materials participants will need to use during the workshop so they can download them in advance. Send only materials they need before and during the workshop; if you plan to send anything for use after the workshop, send it after the workshop is over.

* *Ask participants to inform colleagues and managers that they will be attending the workshop.* Unlike live, in-person workshops, where people leave their desks or work stations to attend, participants may attend virtual workshops without going anywhere. To avoid being interrupted, participants need to let people know that they will be unavailable for the duration of the workshop. You might also suggest that they take their computers to a private space such as a conference room.

3. Gaining Managers' Support

Check What You Know

Which statements about managers' support for training are accurate?

1. _____ Managers who do not recognize the value of training sometimes pull participants out of workshops at the last minute.
2. _____ Managers can support training by making it clear to employees that they expect them to do well in the workshop.
3. _____ Managers should not discuss the training ahead of time with employees because they might have a biased perspective.
4. _____ After the workshop, managers can support training by providing employees with opportunities to use what they learned.
5. _____ Like workshop participants, managers need to know how the training will benefit them.

Keep Participants' Managers Informed

The more support that participants' managers provide both before and after a workshop, the more successful the training is likely to be. In an ideal world, participants' managers fully support the training effort; in the real world, however, that support is not always forthcoming. Managers who do not recognize the value of training and the role it plays in helping their team achieve its goals may see training as taking time away from the participants' "real" work and be quick to pull people out of workshops the moment that something they consider more important comes along. Those managers may not provide opportunities for participants to use what they've learned when they return to their jobs—in fact, they might even block their employees' efforts to make changes. Even managers who believe that the training is important and necessary may not know what they can do to support the process.

Like participants, managers want an answer to the question, "What's in it for me?" They need to know how the training will improve employees' performance and increase their productivity; reduce problems; help them retain valued people; and help them achieve business results. The better their understanding of the value of the training, the more likely they are to support it.

If you can, meet in person or on the phone with participants' managers before a workshop. Clarify the purpose and objectives for the workshop, discuss what they expect training to achieve, help them understand how the training will be useful to them and their employees, and suggest ways in which they can prepare employees for training and support their efforts to apply the learning on the job.

If you are unable to talk directly to managers, communicate with them by e-mail. Send them a description of the program that includes why it is being held, what it is intended to achieve, and the benefits for them and their employees. Make sure that they know when and where the workshop will be held, and how long their employees will be away from work. Keep them up-to-date by sending them copies of the material you send participants, such as questionnaires, assessments, and pre-work assignments. One caution, however: Do not send managers copies of correspondence you have with individual participants or the participants' responses to questionnaires, assessments, or pre-work assignments without the participants' knowledge and agreement.

THINK ABOUT IT

What are some things that managers can do to prepare their employees for training and help them apply what they learn when they are back on the job?

_____

_____

_____

_____

_____

_____

Help Managers Support the Training Effort

Explain to managers that people generally take workshops more seriously and will be better able to learn when they know that their managers consider the training important. To help managers support the training effort, you can offer the suggestions below for helping to prepare their employees for training and them apply the learning when they are back on the job.

Before the Workshop

- Meet with their employees before the workshop to discuss the importance of the training for the employee, the manager, and the organization.
- Help employees clarify their expectations and objectives for training.
- Set up a post-workshop meeting to discuss what the employees learned and identify ways in which the manager can help them apply what they learned.

After the Workshop

- Meet to discuss how what the employees learned relates to their jobs.
- Help employees identify specific changes they want to make as a result of training, develop an action plan, and determine what the manager can do to support change.
- Meet regularly with employees to discuss their progress, identify challenges, and acknowledge their successes.

Quick Quiz

List the three to five key learning points from this chapter that will be most helpful to you.

_____

_____

_____

_____

_____

What's Next?

One of the important tasks in the preparation process is preparing the materials and supplies you need to run the workshop. That process can be very time-consuming, and it takes a plan to make sure that everything gets done, and done right. That's what will be covered in the next chapter.

Apply What You Learn

Answer these questions to determine how you will prepare participants for your workshop.

1. How will workshop participants be (or how have they been) selected?

_____

_____

2. What do participants already know about the workshop? What information do they need?

Already Know	Need to Know
_____	_____
_____	_____
_____	_____
_____	_____
_____	_____
_____	_____

3. What pre-work assignment or assignments will you use?

_____

_____

4. How will you contact the participants' managers? What information do they need?

_____

_____

_____

5. List the talking points for a discussion with the managers.

_____

_____

_____

_____

_____

6. On a separate piece of paper or your computer, draft a "welcome" e-mail.

Answers to Exercises

Check What You Know

Which of the following statements about notifying participants are accurate?

1. ___ The only really important information that participants need about a workshop is the date, the location, and the time.
2. _X_ The way in which participants are notified about training should be the start of a positive learning experience.
3. ___ As long as a manager has given participants all the pertinent information about the workshop, it is not necessary to get in touch with them yourself.

(Continued)

4. _X_ One of the most important things that people want to know about training is how what they will learn will benefit them.
5. ___ An introductory e-mail from you is not appropriate for a workshop that people are required to attend.

Check What You Know

Which of the following would be useful pre-work assignments for a workshop on being a better manager?

1. ___ Ask participants to read the book on which the training program is based and come prepared to discuss it in the workshop.
2. _X_ Ask participants to think of the best manager they have ever known, list the characteristics that made that person a good manager, and bring the list to the workshop.
3. _X_ Ask participants to complete an assessment of their own management strengths and challenges.
4. ___ Ask participants to prepare a biographical report about a successful manager.

Check What You Know

Which are effective strategies for making it more likely that participants will complete a pre-work assignment?

1. _X_ Keep the assignment brief and relevant.
2. ___ Make sure that the assignment will be a lot of fun to do.
3. ___ Explain that you will be giving participants' managers the names of the people who complete the pre-work assignment.
4. _X_ Explain how the pre-work will be used during the workshop.
5. _X_ Ask people to send you something when they have completed the assignment.
6. ___ Make the assignment as challenging as possible.

Check What You Know

Suppose you were planning a virtual workshop, which participants would attend on a website, using audio links to communicate with you and with one another. Which of the statements below about preparing participants for virtual training are accurate?

1. ___ Because most people enjoy computer-based training, it's not as important to prepare them for a virtual workshop as for a live, in-person workshop.
2. _X_ One reason for making a personal contact with participants before the virtual workshop is that you will not have the advantage of face-to-face contact to establish rapport at the beginning of the workshop.
3. ___ It's not usually helpful to use pre-work for a virtual workshop because few people will do it.
4. ___ These days, you can expect that nearly everyone understands the technology and how to use the virtual workshop tools.
5. _X_ If participants will need handouts or other documents during the workshop, send them out in advance.

Check What You Know

Which statements about managers' support for training are accurate?

1. _X_ Managers who do not recognize the value of training sometimes pull participants out of workshops at the last minute.
2. ___ Managers can support training by making it clear to employees that they expect them to do well in the workshop.
3. ___ Managers should not discuss the training ahead of time with employees because they might have a biased perspective.
4. _X_ After the workshop, managers can support training by providing employees with opportunities to use what they learned.
5. _X_ Like workshop participants, managers need to know how the training will benefit them.

4
Preparing Materials and Supplies

When I started out as a trainer, I used to rush around a day or two before the workshop making copies, assembling workbooks, scouring the storeroom for writing tablets and pens, tracking down videos, running out to the store for props, preparing flip-chart pages, and packing everything up. By the time I lugged the boxes into the training room, I'd be exhausted. And sometimes I'd unpack only to find that something important was missing, forcing me to improvise, or worse, to skip activities because I didn't have the necessary materials.

After I while, I got it: running a workshop without the right materials and supplies is like putting on a birthday party without the cake, the party favors, and the games. Getting everything ready wasn't a job that I could leave for the last minute, not if I wanted it done right so I could arrive at the workshop with the confident feeling that comes from knowing that everything is ready to go. Not if I wanted to focus my attention on preparing the participants and myself for training instead of on masking tape and marking pens.

Here's what's in this chapter:

- What to consider about materials and supplies
- What you'll need
- Why and how to use a checklist
- Guidelines for preparing materials and supplies
- The importance of having a backup plan

When we walk into a seminar or workshop and we see a lot of neat "stuff," we start the seminar with the feeling that there's going to be something here for us to benefit from.

Bob Pike, *Creative Training Techniques*

1. What to Consider About Materials and Supplies

Check What You Know

Below are descriptions of how two trainers went about the process of preparing materials and supplies for their workshops. Which trainer is most likely to convey to participants a sense that the workshop should be taken seriously, the day is going to go well, and he or she is knowledgeable and credible? Why?

1. _____ A week before the workshop, Alysha prepares the participant handouts. After checking to make sure that they are attractive, easy to use, and error-free, she has them duplicated and spiral-bound into workbooks. While the workbooks are being produced, she collects and packs the various materials and supplies the workshop requires and stores them in a corner of her office. She creates three prepared flip-chart pages, rolls them into a tube, and puts them with the boxes. On the morning of the workshop, she arrives an hour early so she can unpack the boxes and get everything ready before the participants arrive.

2. _____ The day before the workshop, Marilee goes to the supply room and collects some writing tablets and pens, which she puts into a box with the handouts she has photocopied the previous day. On her way home, she stops at the mall to buy some gadgets that she needs for an opening activity. The next morning, she arrives thirty minutes early so she can collate the handouts and get everything ready. While she is unpacking, she realizes that she has forgotten the name tents, but that's okay—people can use a folded-up a piece of paper. She sees that the time is getting short, so she decides to prepare the flip-chart pages she needs instead of collating the handouts, which she can pass around the room in stacks as they are needed. She is still writing on the flip-chart pages when the participants start to arrive, and it is not until she begins the workshop that she realizes she left the gadgets for the opening activity on her kitchen table at home.

It's amazing how many things you need to run a workshop, from participant handouts and trainer materials to masking tape and marking pens. All that "stuff" has to be produced, purchased, prepared, or obtained. Pulling it together isn't the most exciting or interesting part of a trainer's job—which might be one reason that many trainers never get around to doing it until the last minute.

But the way a trainer handles materials and supplies conveys an indelible impression of the workshop and the trainer to the participants. When trainers like Marilee leave everything to the last minute, they are likely to convey a sense of disorganization and lack of attention that implies they are not taking the workshop very seriously—or that they don't know what they are doing—and that the day is not going to go well. That kind of disorganization distracts participants from the learning process and keeps the workshop from flowing as smoothly as it should.

Trainers like Alysha, on the other hand, who pay attention to the preparation process and are ready to go when participants arrive, appear more credible. The participants are more likely to have a sense that the trainer cares about the workshop and takes it seriously—and so should they.

The process of preparing the materials and supplies is too important to be left for last and done haphazardly. Here are some guidelines for making sure that you have everything you need, that participants perceive you as organized and professional, and that the materials and supplies support the learning process instead of distracting from it.

- Leave enough time in your schedule so you can put everything together without cutting corners, sacrificing quality, or forgetting things that are important to the learning process.

- Use a checklist and a to-do list to keep yourself organized.

- Make sure that the participant handouts present a professional image and are easy to use.

- If you are using anything that needs to be ordered, such as a DVD or a game, order it well ahead of time.

- Keep a box of basic supplies filled and ready to go so you don't have to start from scratch for every workshop.

- If other people are helping you prepare any of the materials or collect supplies, make sure they know what you need and when you need it.

- Leave some extra time in case there are delays in producing materials or obtaining something that need to be ordered.

- Make a backup plan, just in case something fails to arrive or turns out to be missing on workshop day.

2. Why and How to Use a Checklist

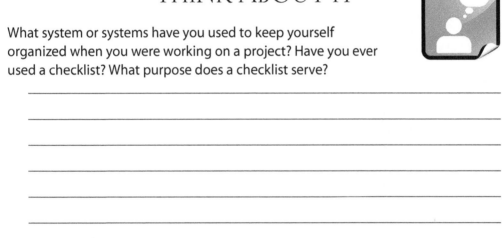

THINK ABOUT IT

What system or systems have you used to keep yourself organized when you were working on a project? Have you ever used a checklist? What purpose does a checklist serve?

_____

_____

_____

_____

_____

_____

Some trainers keep themselves organized by using to-do lists or pop-up reminders, or by putting Post-it Notes up on the wall over their computers. Some make a detailed project plan that tracks the progress of every item they need. But what works best for many trainers is a checklist like the one that Leon mentioned to Cybelle. Although you won't use exactly the same checklist for each workshop—in one, you might only need a few handouts and some basic supplies, while in another you will need professionally produced participant workbooks, videos, and a variety of props—you can create a template for yourself and adapt it for different situations.

Your checklist will be more useful if you organize items into the general categories into which they tend to fall:

- Basic supplies
- Participant materials
- Trainer materials
- Audiovisual materials
- Materials for activities
- Administrative materials

What You'll Need

BASIC MATERIALS

- Name tents
- Writing tablets
- Pens and pencils
- Marking pens for flip charts
- Dry Erase markers for whiteboards
- Tape and push pins for posting flip-chart pages
- Paper clips and a stapler
- Post-it Notes

PARTICIPANT MATERIALS

- Handouts and/or participant workbooks
- Job aids
- Evaluation forms
- Reference materials

TRAINER MATERIALS

- Trainer notes, trainer guide, and/or script
- At-a-glance agenda
- Laser pointer for slides
- Watch or small clock for managing the time

MATERIALS FOR ACTIVITIES
- Case studies
- Self-assessments
- Props
- Index cards
- Post-it Notes and/or colored dots
- Materials for games
- Colored pens or crayons

AUDIOVISUAL MATERIALS
- Slides or laptop with PowerPoint presentation
- DVDs and/or CDs
- Prepared flip-chart pages
- Wall posters
- Models

ADMINISTRATIVE MATERIALS
- Participant list or roster
- Sign-in sheets
- Feedback forms
- Certificates of completion

Here are some steps you can follow to develop and use a checklist:

1. As soon as you know that you will be conducting a workshop, make a list of everything that you will need. Make the list in the form of a checklist, with boxes to check off when things are ready. Organize the list so that it makes sense to you. Include the quantity of each item that you will need. If you make the list on your computer, print it out so that you can keep a copy close at hand. Leave space to add items as needed.

2. Indicate where each item will come from. Does it need to be ordered from a supplier? Located in a supply room? Purchased at a store?

Professionally developed and produced? Downloaded from a computer, printed out, and assembled? Indicate who will be responsible for producing or obtaining each item. If it's someone else, make sure that person knows exactly what you need and when you need it.

3. Indicate when each item needs to be ready. Leave some extra time when setting deadlines. Also decide what happens with items when they are ready. Will you store them in your office or somewhere else? Will they be shipped or delivered to the training site?

4. Review the list every day. Check off items when they are ready. Cross off any items that you realize you won't need and add any that you hadn't thought of at first. Check the progress on items that others are producing or providing. Redo the checklist if necessary so it is legible and easy to use.

> ## To Keep Yourself Organized
>
> - Make a checklist that shows everything that you will need, organized into categories.
> - Indicate where each item will come from, who is responsible for producing or obtaining it, and when it needs to be ready.
> - Review and update the list every day.

5. Stay on top of the process by putting action items on your daily to-do list. Your goal should be to have everything packed up and ready to go a few days before the workshop—sooner if things need to be shipped to the training site.

There's a sample checklist at the end of the chapter.

3. Guidelines for Preparing Materials and Supplies

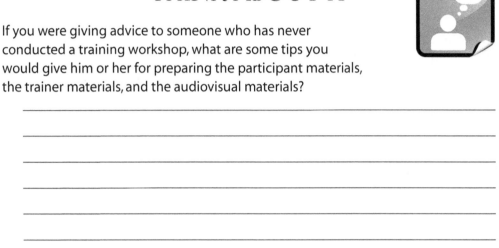

THINK ABOUT IT

If you were giving advice to someone who has never conducted a training workshop, what are some tips you would give him or her for preparing the participant materials, the trainer materials, and the audiovisual materials?

_____

_____

_____

_____

_____

_____

Participant Materials

As a trainer, you will not always be responsible for designing and developing the handouts that provide participants with information, reinforce the learning points, and are used for activities. For some workshops, in fact, you will use a training package that includes professionally produced participant workbooks or master copies of handouts, ready to be duplicated. But for other workshops, you will need to develop and produce the participant handouts or workbook yourself. Even when you use a professionally produced training package, you might want to create some additional handouts so you can fit the workshop more closely to the participants' specific needs. Here are some suggestions for making sure that any handouts you create are professional in appearance and easy to use.

- Make sure that handouts are neat and error-free. Sloppy handouts that are filled with typos convey the message that the workshop isn't very important. It's not necessary to spend a lot of time and money on fancy graphic designs—in fact, too many graphics and fancy formatting can

Do They Really Need All That Information?

Have you ever attended a workshop in which the trainer gave you a huge binder, stuffed with information? Not only is lifting a binder of that size a chore, it's pretty useless when it comes to training. It's unwieldy. It's hard to turn the pages. Even with a good table of contents and lot of tabs, it's hard to find things. And for reference after the workshop ... forget it. Binders of that size go up on a shelf where they stay until you clean out your office.

If you have so many handouts that they fill a large binder, stop and reconsider. Do participants really need all that information? Which pages will they actually use during the workshop? Take all the pages they will use out of the binder and assemble them into a packet, folder, or binder of manageable size. If they'll need the rest of the information after the workshop, package it separately and give it to them as they leave. Better yet, send it to them later or put it on a website.

make materials difficult to use. Keep handouts simple, use formatting that makes it easy for participants to grasp the information, and proofread carefully for errors before printing or duplicating them.

- Make sure that handouts are easy to use. Trainers often give out handouts as they use them during the workshop, but I've found that too many loose handouts only end up scattered all over the tables and the floor. Unless you are using only a few handouts—I'd say five or six at the most—staple them into a packet or assemble them into a folder, a binder, or a spiral-bound workbook and give them to participants at the beginning of the workshop. Number the pages and, if necessary, include tabs and a table of contents so people can quickly find what they need.

- Make sure you have enough handouts for all the participants. It's not uncommon for trainers to discover that they don't have quite enough handouts or participant workbooks. That might be an admirable effort to save trees, but it means that some participants will have to share unless more copies can be made on the spot. Check to see that you will have enough for everyone, and bring a couple of extra copies, just in case.

Delivering Training Workshops: Pfeiffer Essential Guides to Training Basics.
Copyright © 2010 by John Wiley & Sons, Inc.
Reproduced by permission of Pfeiffer, an Imprint of Wiley. www.Pfeiffer.com

Trainer Materials

The trainer materials are anything you will need to be able to deliver the workshop. You might plan to use a trainer package that includes a detailed script, or you might need to make your own script or notes. You might need to bring reference books or manuals or put reference material on your laptop so that you can answer questions that come up during the workshop.

Make sure that the materials you will use to facilitate the workshop are formatted and packaged so that you can use them easily. Decide what you need to hold in your hands while you are presenting information or leading a discussion. Some trainers prefer to put key information on index cards instead of holding a binder or single sheets of paper.

If you're using a detailed script, you will probably want to make an outline or an at-a-glance agenda that lists all the activities and includes key content points, or you might want to create a script for yourself on the Notes pages of your PowerPoint presentation. Practice with different types of trainer materials and see what works best for you.

Audiovisual Materials

Audiovisual materials such as a slide presentation, videos, prepared flip-chart pages, and CDs can be very important to the success of your workshop. Like error-filled handouts, sloppy audiovisual materials imply that the training isn't important enough to be worth the trouble of doing them right.

If you are using a PowerPoint presentation, remember that the point of the visuals is to support your presentation, not to replace it. Check to be sure that the slides are consistent in format and legible from the back of the room, and that they don't have too many busy graphics that distract from the message. Delete any slides that won't be needed so you don't have to click through them during the workshop—it can be very annoying when slides appear momentarily and then disappear. If you plan to post any prepared flip-chart pages, prepare them in advance so that you won't be working on them when participants arrive.

Materials for Activities

Your checklist should include all the materials you need to conduct the learning activities. Some of those materials, such as case studies and questions for small-group discussions, might be included in the participant handouts or workbooks. But some activities require things that need to be ordered, such as videos, software, or assessments; others require ordinary things that need to be obtained or purchased, such as bells, timers, chalk, sticky tape, toys, and more. Still others require things that need to be fabricated, such as game boards. Be sure to identify everything that you will need and leave enough time to obtain or create each item—missing materials might mean that you'll have to skip an activity. Also, when you pack up for the workshop, think about how and when you will use each item. For example, you will probably want to put the things that will be used in the opening activity at the top, not at the bottom, of a box.

Administrative Materials

The "stuff" you need for a workshop is likely to include some administrative material, such as participant lists and rosters, sign-in sheets, evaluation questionnaires, and certificates of completion. I find that these are the easiest materials to forget because they are not directly involved in the delivery of the workshop. But they are important, nevertheless. Be sure to include them on your checklist and get them ready early so you don't have to think about them at the last minute.

Basic Supplies

Like the administrative materials, it's easy to forget about basic supplies. But not having such things as tape to post flip-chart pages and marking pens that still have a good supply of ink can drive you crazy on workshop day. That's why I suggest keeping a box in your office with the supplies that you are likely to need for all your workshops. Keeping those things handy saves you the time and trouble of gathering them over and over again. Replenish your stash after each workshop so that you don't have to think about those things again until it comes time to pack up for the next one.

Here's what a basic supplies box might include:

- Name tags or name "tents," which can be four-by-six-inch index cards folded in half lengthwise
- Writing tablets and pens or pencils (check the pens for ink and sharpen the pencils)
- Marking pens for flip charts and/or erasable markers for whiteboard (check marking pens and erasable markers after each workshop and throw away any that have run dry)

- Masking tape, painter's tape, and/or push pins for posting flip-chart pages (unless you will be using flip-chart paper that sticks to the wall—although bring some tape or pins anyway in case the sticky stuff doesn't work, which is often the case)

- Stapler and paper clips (check the stapler to be sure that it's full)

- Post-it Notes of various sizes and colors

- An extra bulb for the projector, just in case

- Extra batteries for equipment such as laser pointers and remote controls

- Cables for hooking up your laptop to the projector

- One or more extension cords

- Electrician's tape for taping down extension cords

About Colored Marking Pens

There are a few things to keep in mind about the marking pens you'll use to write on flip-chart pages and whiteboards:

- They are not interchangeable—the pens commonly used for flip-chart pages do not erase from whiteboards, at least not easily. Use only pens designed for whiteboards for whiteboards.
- Use water-based marking pens for flip-chart pages, not permanent markers. Some trainers like permanent markers because the color is richer. But permanent markers bleed through the paper, and if you forget yourself and write on your clothing (as I have done from time to time), you'll never get it off.
- Avoid red, yellow, and orange, except for highlighting. Those colors are hard to see from the back of the room. Keep a few of the red, yellow, and orange pens that come in the boxes and give the rest to your kids to play with.
- Throw pens away as soon as the ink starts to run out so you do not find them among the good pens the next time you do a workshop.

Delivering Training Workshops: Pfeiffer Essential Guides to Training Basics.
Copyright © 2010 by John Wiley & Sons, Inc.
Reproduced by permission of Pfeiffer, an Imprint of Wiley. www.Pfeiffer.com

Preparing Materials and Supplies

4. Make a Backup Plan

I think that all trainers should post those words on a banner above their computers. No matter how careful you are about preparing materials and supplies, chances are that something will be missing or something will go wrong. So think about what you will do if the DVD you ordered doesn't arrive, the printer doesn't finish the participant workbooks on time, the slide presentation is accidentally deleted from your flash drive, the box you shipped gets lost, or the training facility delivers flip-chart pads with only five sheets of paper. Knowing that you have backup plans keeps you from worrying and makes it easier to cope if something does go wrong.

Preparing Materials for Virtual Workshops

Although you need fewer materials for a virtual workshop, it is even more important that the materials be clear, easy-to-use, and professional in appearance. The materials, especially the visuals, "carry" more of the content in a virtual workshop than in a live, in-person workshop where people are communicating face-to-face.

The materials you'll need include visuals, such as slides, video clips, documents, charts, and graphs that will be shared with the participants during the workshop; materials for pre-work, such as case studies or assessments; handouts that will be used during the workshop; and materials that participants will receive after the workshop.

Make sure that all the visuals are ready and have been tested well ahead of time so you can make any necessary changes. Send out pre-work materials or links to those materials when you notify participants about the training. Send handouts—note-taking pages, worksheets, key learning points, and other information people need to use or refer to during the workshop—a few days in advance so participants can download them. Wait to send any supplementary information until the workshop is over.

Quick Quiz

List the three to five key learning points from this chapter that will be most helpful to you.

_____

_____

_____

_____

_____

What's Next?

You've prepared the participants, and you have all the materials and supplies ready. But there is one more task that is crucial to the success of your workshop: preparing yourself. That's what you'll learn about in the next chapter.

Apply What You Learn

Make a materials and supplies checklist for your workshop. You can use the checklist at the end of the chapter or use that checklist as a model for one of your own.

Answers to Exercise

Check What You Know

Below are descriptions of how two trainers went about the process of preparing materials and supplies for their workshops. Which trainer is most likely to convey to participants a sense that the workshop should be taken seriously, the day is going to go well, and he or she is knowledgeable and credible? Why?

1. __X__ A week before the workshop, Alysha prepares the participant handouts. After checking to make sure that they are attractive, easy to use, and error-free and she has them duplicated and spiral-bound into workbooks. While the workbooks are being produced, she collects and packs the various materials and supplies the workshop requires and stores them in a corner of her office. She creates three prepared flip-chart pages, rolls them into a tube, and puts them with the boxes. On the morning of the workshop, she arrives an hour early so she can unpack the boxes and get everything ready before the participants arrive.

2. _____ The day before the workshop, Marilee goes to the supply room and collects some writing tablets and pens, which she puts into a box with the handouts she has photocopied the previous day. On her way home, she stops at the mall to buy some gadgets that she needs for an opening activity. The next morning, she arrives thirty minutes early so she can collate the handouts and get everything ready. While she is unpacking, she realizes that she forgotten the name tents, but that's okay—people can use a folded-up a piece of paper. She sees that the time is getting short, so she decides to prepare the flip-chart pages she needs instead of collating the handouts, which she can pass around the room in stacks as they are needed. She is still writing on the flip-chart pages when the participants start to arrive, and it is not until she begins the workshop that she realizes she left the gadgets for the opening activity on her kitchen table at home.

Delivering Training Workshops: Pfeiffer Essential Guides to Training Basics.
Copyright © 2010 by John Wiley & Sons, Inc.
Reproduced by permission of Pfeiffer, an Imprint of Wiley. www.Pfeiffer.com

Because she has paid attention to the preparation process and is ready to go when participants arrive, Alysha is likely to appear more credible, conveying the sense that she takes the workshop seriously—and so should the participants. By leaving everything to the last minute, Marilee is likely to convey a sense of disorganization and lack of attention that implies she does not take the workshop very seriously—or doesn't know what she doing; her disorganization can be distracting to participants.

Materials and Supplies Checklist

Workshop Title: _____

Workshop Date: _____

Item	Source	Responsibility	Deadline	Notes
☐				
☐				
☐				
☐				
☐				
☐				

5
Preparing Yourself

Check What You Know

Workshop day is approaching. Cybelle has worked hard to make sure that the participants are well-prepared and that everything will be ready. "I'm feeling a little nervous," she admitted to Leon. "I really want to do a good job. Is there anything else that I should be doing?"

"It's normal to feel nervous the first time you run a workshop," Leon told her. "Making sure that you've done everything on your checklist will help, because you'll know that you're ready. But it's also important to prepare yourself. The more prepared you are, the more confident and relaxed you'll be when people walk into the room on workshop day."

What advice do you think Leon gave Cybelle about preparing herself so she is ready for the workshop?

_____

_____

_____

_____

_____

_____

Years ago, when I was a volunteer with a community theater group, I was asked to step in at the last minute for someone who was to present an important proposal to a foundation funding committee. The first time I saw the proposal was in the lobby fifteen minutes before the appointment with the committee. I had just enough time to glance through it quickly and make a few notes. I knew that the grant we hoped to obtain would provide nearly half of our support for the coming year, and I had misgivings about making such an important presentation when I knew so little, to a group about which I knew even less. But I'm an experienced trainer, I reminded myself—how hard could it be?

But when I stood up before the group, my hands began to shake and my mouth was so dry I could hardly get the words out to introduce myself. "Could you please speak up?" someone at the back asked, not unkindly. "Of course," I said, forcing myself to speak more loudly, although it felt as if I was shouting. The presentation went downhill from there. Instead of presenting highlights from the proposal, which I had not had time to extract, I read it to the group, word for word, even though all the committee members had copies. Knowing that I had limited time, I began reading faster and faster, looking frantically for sections that I could skip. Finally, a woman raised her hand: "Excuse me for interrupting," she said, "but we've all read the proposal. The purpose of our meeting today was to ask questions so we could make a decision about whether to fund your programs." I could feel the heat rising in my face as I squared my shoulders and said, "Of course." And then they started asking questions—questions that I had no idea how to answer.

The information in this chapter can help you avoid those kinds of experiences when you deliver training. You'll find:

- A personal preparation primer
- The importance of getting to know the workshop
- How to learn more about the subject
- How to feel more comfortable with the audience
- Reasons for thinking about your appearance
- How to practice your delivery

1. A Personal Preparation Primer

How you come across to your participants is just as important as your training design and content. In fact, because you are the medium through which the message is communicated, your demeanor, appearance, and behavior can make or break a program.

Karen Lawson, *The Trainer's Handbook* (2nd ed.)

Check What You Know

Which of the statements about presentation fear, or "stage fright" are accurate?

1. _____ Symptoms of anxiety and nervousness are a natural human reaction to stress.
2. _____ For nearly everyone, the symptoms of "stage fright" disappear with sufficient experience.
3. _____ The most effective way to prevent or reduce anxiety and nervousness is to memorize the workshop script, word for word.
4. _____ Establishing rapport with the participants can help to reduce symptoms of nervousness.
5. _____ Being well prepared makes you less prone to symptoms of nervousness because it increases your sense of confidence.

Stage fright is the fear of putting ourselves out there in front of other people who might judge us and find us lacking. Teachers get it, presenters get it, corporate speakers get it, successful actors get it. The best, most experienced trainers get it. The symptoms of stage fright can take you completely by surprise—you're feeling great, ready to deliver a dynamic workshop, and suddenly your hands are shaking, your legs feel like rubber, and your throat is so dry you can hardly croak, "Good morning."

A Natural Human Reaction

Symptoms of anxiety and nervousness, such as dry mouth, sweating, increased heart rate, rapid and shallow breathing, tense shoulder and stomach muscles, shaking hands, and Silly Putty legs are part of our body's defenses against stress, and you can't make them disappear by strength of will alone. Sometimes called "flight or fight" responses, they are similar to those you might experience if you met up with a bear on a camping trip.

Not all trainers experience these symptoms, and even those who do find that they diminish with experience. But the physical symptoms of stress can strike without warning, especially in unfamiliar and high-stakes situations. Trying to ignore them can actually make them worse, so it's important to learn what you can do to reduce their likelihood and cope with the symptoms when they do appear.

The Gallup organization, among others, has found that nearly half the population has a fear of speaking in public that is greater than their fear of almost anything else—snakes, heights, you name it. Among trainers, some experience the anxiety and nervousness that can accompany the delivery of a workshop only rarely, if ever, but many others never lose it completely, no matter how many workshops they've delivered.

Fortunately, there are tried-and-tested strategies that you can use to reduce your presentation fear and cope with its symptoms. First and foremost is to be as prepared as possible. It's preparation that helps you relax and gives you the confidence you need to make a positive first impression, establish rapport, gain participants' trust, and maintain an environment that is conducive to learning.

Here's an overview of what you need to do to prepare yourself for training. In the rest of this chapter, we will examine each of these activities more closely.

- *Get to know the workshop.* I've known trainers who went "onstage" without doing much more than flipping through the trainer's guide, then were surprised when they felt nervous, had trouble remembering what came next, and received low ratings from participants on "knowledge of subject" and "able to keep things moving smoothly." Preparation starts by studying the workshop until you thoroughly understand the content, structure, and activities. The better your understanding, the more confident and relaxed you will feel and the easier it will be to keep things running smoothly.

Become familiar with the subject. Feeling unsure about your knowledge of the subject matter can make you feel anxious about the workshop. If you are using a well-designed training program, you don't have to be an expert in the subject matter to be able to help people learn. But you should know enough about the subject so that you can use the trainer materials to answer participants' questions. If the trainer's guide doesn't provide enough information, do some research, read up on the subject, and look for subject-matter experts who can explain things that are not clear to you and help you get up-to-speed.

Learn about the audience. One reason that trainers experience pre-workshop anxiety and symptoms of stage fright is that they don't know enough about the participants. It can be intimidating to stand up in front of an "audience"; it's much less anxiety-provoking to stand up in front of a group of other human beings. Learning something about the jobs that participants do, why they are there, what they expect, and what concerns they have about the training helps you see them as people and makes it much easier to establish rapport quickly.

Think about your appearance. First impressions are important—we all make snap judgments about people based on their clothing and personal grooming, so we feel more confident and comfortable when we think we look our best. Get started on the right foot by choosing the right clothes and paying attention to your personal appearance.

Practice. An understudy who has to jump into a theatrical role with little preparation will make more mistakes and feel less confident than one who has rehearsed for weeks before opening night. Practicing your delivery helps you manage the anxiety and nervousness that so often plague both new and experienced trainers. Later in this chapter you'll find suggestions to help you practice.

Delivering Training Workshops: Pfeiffer Essential Guides to Training Basics.
Copyright © 2010 by John Wiley & Sons, Inc.
Reproduced by permission of Pfeiffer, an Imprint of Wiley. www.Pfeiffer.com

2. Getting to Know the Workshop

Check What You Know

Suppose you were asked to deliver your organization's orientation workshop for new hires. The date has been set and the participants have already been notified. Now you need to prepare yourself to conduct the training. Your manager has given you a package that includes a trainer's guide with a workshop script, a participant workbook, and the slide presentation. What could you do to get to know this workshop?

_____

_____

_____

_____

_____

_____

Sometimes you will have intimate knowledge about a workshop because you were closely involved in its development. But you will often deliver workshops that other people have designed and developed. To deliver one of those workshops successfully, you need to spend some time getting to know the objectives, content, activities, and structure as thoroughly as possible.

The best way to get to know a workshop is to experience it yourself as a participant or an observer—you'll not only learn the content and become familiar with the activities and materials, but you'll see how the participants interact with the trainer and one another and hear the kinds of questions that people ask. If someone in your organization or in another organization is delivering the same workshop, ask whether you can attend and arrange a time to talk with the trainer afterward. Those opportunities aren't always available, but be sure to take advantage of them when they are.

Even if you do have a chance to attend a workshop before you deliver it yourself, you will still need to study all the materials carefully. Begin by reading all the trainer and participant materials through quickly, and then read them again, more slowly the second time. Then go through everything again, and again, as often as needed to feel comfortable that you know it. As you read, examine the ways in which the activities, visuals, and participant handouts or workbook relate to one another. Use a highlighter to mark key points. Note questions you have about the content, structure, or activities, anything for which you need more information, anything that you don't completely understand. If the materials do not include an agenda or a script, develop your own.

3. Learning More About the Subject

Check What You Know

The training package your manager provided contains everything you'll need to run the new hire orientation workshop, including a detailed agenda and a script. But even after studying all the materials carefully, you feel that you need to know more about the subject. What could you do to learn more?

_____

_____

_____

_____

One of the things that's great about training is the opportunity to learn about lots of different subjects. Chances are that you will not be an expert in the subjects that you teach—few trainers are. But to feel confident that you can explain the concepts and answer participants' questions, you might need to learn more than what's available in the trainer materials. For example, if I were delivering a workshop on corporate ethics, which I know about mostly from what I read in the newspapers, I would read up on the subject and talk to experts in the field until I felt that I knew enough so I would feel on solid ground when I walked into the training room.

How much time and effort to spend learning more about the subject depends on such factors as what you already know, how complete the training materials are, and the kinds of questions that participants are likely to ask during the workshop. Here are some ways in which you can learn more:

- *Read up on the subject.* Look for books, articles, and other resource material that will help you increase your understanding, clarify concepts and information that you do not fully understand, and offer ideas and techniques that might be helpful for your participants. You can find lots of information by doing a web search and following links that seem likely to lead you to useful resources.

- *Attend a presentation, seminar, college class, or workshop.* If you have the time and the inclination, this can be a great way to learn more about a subject that you will be teaching. But courses and workshops can be costly and take a lot of time, so check out the description, the learning objectives, the agenda, and the teacher or trainer's qualifications carefully to make sure that you'll get what you need.

- *Watch a video, attend a web-based seminar, or listen to a podcast.* An increasing number of training topics are being addressed in online workshops, e-learning programs, and web-based seminars, some of which are available free or at a low cost. One way to learn about these kinds of offerings is to sign up for e-mail newsletters from professional organizations.

- *Consult with subject-matter experts.* An excellent way to learn more about a subject that you'll

About Subject-Matter Experts

There are two types of subject-matter experts: those who have a great deal of knowledge about a particular subject (such as the laws related to conducting job interviews) and those who have a great deal of knowledge about how to do something (such as how to build a website). Subject-matter experts can give you extremely valuable information, but they can also lead you in the wrong direction. Make sure you know what you're looking for and that you work with subject-matter experts who can give you accurate and complete information about the subject or about the way that something is supposed to be done.

be teaching is to talk with someone who knows a lot about it. Subject-matter experts are particularly helpful when the workshop is focused on company-specific content, such as policies, procedures, and processes. Be sure to choose people who can give you the right information, and come armed with a list of questions to make the best use of the person's time.

4. Learning More About the Audience

Check What You Know

You know that the people who will be attending the new hire orientation are in their first month of work for the company, and you have a roster with their names and their positions. But that's about it. What else would be helpful to know about the audience? How could you find more information?

_____

_____

_____

_____

_____

_____

Certain types of audiences make a trainer quake in her proverbial boots: those who are far more knowledgeable and/or more senior in the organization; those, such as customers, who are very important to the organization; and those who have a reputation for being difficult. It's important to acknowledge and confront any feelings you may have about the prospect of facing the audience so that those feelings do not get in the way of your ability to deliver a dynamic, successful workshop. But keep in mind that knowledge is power: the more you know about the participants, the better able you will be to look at the workshop from their points of view and feel confident that you can deliver it in a way that meets their needs.

For example, I like to know what kinds of work participants do, what positions they hold, how long they've been in their positions, and how long they've been with the organization. I pay particular attention to people who are new to the job and the company, and to those who have been doing the same work for many years. That's because new people might feel unsure of themselves and be reluctant to risk making mistakes or reveal a lack of knowledge, and people with years of experience sometimes feel that there is nothing more they need to learn and resent being in the same workshop as people who are new to the job. Knowing that there will be people from both groups in the same workshop, I can take advantage of the situation by using activities that help the newer people learn from those who are more experienced and help the people who've been around for a while benefit from the fresh perspectives of those who are new to the job.

The best way to learn about the people who will be attending training is to talk to them directly, either individually or in small groups. Sometimes a conversation will reveal extremely useful information. For example, you might learn that several of the participants took a workshop on the same subject last year and were very disappointed by it or that some participants see training as "punishment" for poor performance. Knowing about those kinds of feelings and perceptions in advance can help you take steps to engage participants who might otherwise resist becoming involved in the learning process.

When you can't talk to individual participants, look for other ways to gather information. As mentioned in Chapter 3, you can use a questionnaire to elicit participants' expectations for and concerns about training. A questionnaire could also elicit such information as the participants' experiences with training, how they see the relationship of the training to their jobs and their professional development, how they were selected for training, and what they already know about the subject.

During conversations with the participants or when you review their responses to your questionnaire, watch for indications that the workshop might not be appropriate for a specific individual—perhaps the person lacks the necessary prerequisites or his or her need for the information differs significantly from those of the others in the group. Also watch for signs that someone's concerns need to be addressed before the workshop. A statement such as, "My manager told me to take this workshop—I don't see the point" or "This workshop comes at a really busy time for me" indicates that you might need to discuss the issue with the person before training begins.

5. Thinking About Your Appearance

Check What You Know

You think that you're just about ready for the new hire orientation workshop when a colleague asks, "What are you going to wear?" What *are* you going to wear? What are some of the things you should think about when deciding how to dress for a workshop?

_____

_____

_____

_____

The first workshop I ever did was a one-day business writing program for a large insurance company. Although I was nervous, I had prepared carefully and the workshop went very smoothly. The participants' evaluations were positive, and my client was pleased. "There's only one thing," she said. "In the future, you might want to dress down a little so that you'll be more approachable—not so 'teacherly.'" I was surprised. I had put some thought into my appearance. In fact, I'd gone out and bought a new outfit specifically for this workshop. But then I realized what she meant. The people in my workshop had worn casual, comfortable business clothing. And there I was, standing up before them in my new, severely cut dark blue business suit.

Most people feel more confident and comfortable when they feel that they look their best and are dressed appropriately for the situation. Whether you are a person who never gives much thought to your clothing or one who enjoys planning what to wear to work every day, it's worthwhile to consider your appearance when you are about to deliver a workshop. People will begin to form an impression of you the moment they walk in the door, so think about what you want them to see.

Consider the following:

- *Choose your clothing ahead of time.* Don't wait until the day of the workshop to think about what you are going to wear—you'll have far more important things to do. If you decide to wear anything other than what you usually wear to work, select your clothes the day before (or earlier) and lay them out so they'll be ready when you get up in the morning with the workshop on your mind.

- *Dress professionally, but appropriately for the group.* If the participants typically wear business suits, wear a business suit. If they typically wear jeans and casual shirts, you might choose more of a "business casual" look.

- *Opt for comfort.* You'll be standing, sitting, and moving around for several hours in those clothes. If your slacks are too tight or your shoes pinch, you'll soon start to feel uncomfortable, and your discomfort is likely to show.

- *Avoid clothing that calls attention to itself.* Participants should see you, not your clothes. Choose simple, neutral styles and colors. If you're a man, leave the Hawaiian shirts, funny ties or T-shirts, baggy pants, and big gold chains at home; if you're a woman, avoid short, tight skirts, overly large or colorful print blouses and dresses, oversized or dangling jewelry, and stiletto heels.

- *Try everything on and move around.* If you plan to wear new clothes or clothing that's much different from what you ordinarily wear to work, try everything on. Check the mirror to make sure that the image you project is what you want participants to see. Walk around, stand, sit, and get up again until you know that you will feel comfortable.

6. Practicing Your Delivery

Check What You Know

Everything is ready for your new hire orientation workshop, and you feel as if you are well prepared. But there is one more thing you need to do—practice.

1. What are some of the payoffs of practicing?

_____

_____

2. How do you know how much practice you need?

_____

_____

3. What are some things you can do to practice?

_____

_____

_____

_____

The old cliché, "practice makes perfect," is essential for success in many endeavors. Practice can be a matter of life and death—we expect (and hope) that surgeons get lots of practice in safe situations before they operate on real live human beings; the same goes for pilots before they are put in charge of a jet filled with hundreds of people. Musicians and opera singers never stop practicing in their quest for perfection; actors put in hours and days of practice before the curtain goes up on a new play. It doesn't take much experience for a trainer to learn that practice pays off in terms of greatly increased self-confidence, far less anxiety and nervousness, and a more successful workshop.

How much practice you'll need depends on such factors as how well you already know the material, how difficult the material is to deliver, the complexity of the activities, the importance of the workshop, and your

To Memorize or Not to Memorize?

Practicing your delivery does not mean memorizing a script. People who give memorized presentations often seem to be looking at the audience, but what they are really looking at is the place behind their eyes where the speech is rolling on an internal teleprompter. Even if there is a detailed, word-for-word script in the trainer's guide, create your own bullet-point summary so that you only need to use the script for reference or content that you need to read aloud.

experience in delivering training. At one end of the spectrum, it's enough to walk through the workshop a few times until you feel that you will be comfortable delivering the key content, giving instructions for activities, making transitions, and using the slides. At the other end, you'll need to pull together some people to act as audience while you do an abbreviated version of the training.

When in doubt, err on the side of too much practice, especially if you are new to training, the material is difficult, and/or the stakes are high. Practice until you feel that you can open the workshop and establish rapport with confidence; deliver the content clearly; introduce, monitor, and debrief all the activities; be flexible enough to respond to participants' specific needs; answer participants' questions; and deal with anything unexpected that might come up.

Here are some suggestions for getting the most out of your practice time.

- *Practice with the trainer materials that you'll use during the workshop.* If you plan to keep the script on a side table for reference and use only an outline during the workshop, use the outline for practice. If you'll be holding the script, or portions of the script, in your hands while you're in front of the group, practice with the script in your hands.

- *Practice out loud.* Reading silently to yourself is not practice—it's reading, and it does little to prepare you to deliver the workshop out loud in front of a group. Further, speaking the words you're going to say in a whisper won't prepare you for speaking in a voice that carries to the back of the room. Instead, find a place where you can practice speaking in full voice so you can get used to the sound. If you plan to use a microphone, practice with the microphone, but also practice without it so you'll be ready in case it malfunctions during the workshop.

- *Practice on your feet.* People who are new to training do not always realize that there is a big difference between talking to a group from a seated position and talking to them while they are seated and you are standing up. You'll feel much more comfortable delivering the workshop on your feet if you practice on your feet.

Practice with the slides, flip charts, other visual aids and media, and any props you will be using. It's not easy to coordinate all the elements of a workshop—to talk while advancing slides at the right moment, record participants' responses to questions on flip-chart pages, use props to illustrate points—so it's important to practice with all the things you'll be using. If you don't have access to a projector for practice, put the slide presentation up on your computer. Start and stop the DVDs at the right points in the presentation. Set up a flip-chart easel and record some of the points that participants are likely to make during the discussions.

Practice in the clothes you'll be wearing. That's especially important if they are different from your ordinary, everyday clothes. People tend to carry themselves differently when they are dressed in formal business clothing than when they are wearing jeans and tennis shoes. If you're pulling your rarely worn business suit and dress shoes out of the closet for this workshop, wear them while you practice.

If possible, practice in front of other people. Imagining that you are delivering the workshop to real people is one thing; actually delivering it to live human beings is another. If you're new to training, or if the workshop is difficult to deliver for one reason or another, ask a few colleagues to be your audience while you deliver a condensed version of the workshop. Focus on key parts, such as the opening, important content, stories, instructions for activities, debriefing questions, transitions, and the closing. Practice answering the kinds of questions that participants are likely to ask. Ask the volunteers to give you feedback: Did you make enough eye contact? Did you speak too quickly? Too softly? How was your diction? Your posture and movement?

> ## Guidelines for Practice
> - Practice with the notes or script that you'll be using.
> - Practice out loud.
> - Practice on your feet.
> - Practice with the visual aids, media, and props you will be using.
> - Practice in the clothes you'll be wearing.
> - Practice in front of other people.
> - Practice in the training room.

- *Practice in the training room.* Practicing in a small space such as your office cubicle or your living room at home is not the same as practicing in the actual training room or in another room that is of similar size and shape. Stand in the trainer area and imagine the participants in their seats while you practice the opening of the workshop. Walk around the room and imagine that you are watching the participants at work on an activity. Think about the questions they are likely to ask and practice answering a few of them. See what it takes for your voice to fill the space.

Check What You Know

Suppose you were advising a colleague who was about to deliver his first virtual workshop. What tips would you give him?

_____

_____

_____

_____

_____

_____

Preparing Yourself to Deliver a Virtual Workshop

Careful preparation and practice are essential for any workshop to run smoothly, and they may be even more important to the successful delivery of a virtual workshop. It's far more difficult to improvise, make changes on the spot, and get back on track if things go off course when you and the learners are linked only by technology. You need to be able to establish a positive learning environment and communicate with participants without the facial expressions and body language that provide such important information when you are with people face-to-face; introduce and conduct activities with people who are not in the same physical space; keep people engaged when their environments are likely to include lots of distractions; and use the technological tools with ease.

Here are some suggestions for preparing yourself to conduct successful virtual training:

- *Learn how virtual training sessions work.* There are a number of important differences between live, in-person workshops and virtual workshops. One of the best ways to learn about those differences is to attend some virtual workshops as a participant. Be sure to attend virtual workshops—synchronous training where participants interact with the trainer and one another—not webinars, which are really video presentations. You can also find tutorials, as well as virtual workshops and webinars, on delivering virtual training. And you can ask the people who manage virtual meeting rooms to explain the process, show you how to use the different tools, and help you practice using them.

- *Practice using the script.* Virtual workshops need to be carefully scripted. If you are using a prepared trainer script or guide, go through it carefully so that you know exactly where you do each action, such as show a visual, ask a polling question, or introduce an activity. If you have no prepared script or guide, make one for yourself.

- *Practice in the virtual training room.* Once you have a good understanding of how to use all the technological tools and have practiced using the script, do at least one dry run in the virtual training room. If possible, ask someone to log on with you and be a "participant" during your practice session. Then go through the workshop as if you were delivering it. Don't skip anything—put up all the slides, write on the whiteboard, ask the questions you plan to ask. If you are going to be "on camera," practice delivering the material from a seated position directly into the camera, without moving around the way you would move if you were addressing a group in a live classroom.

- *The day of the workshop, arrive early, just as you would for any training session.* Make sure that you are in a quiet, private place where you will not be interrupted and that you have everything you need. Arrange your trainer materials where you can refer to them easily without shuffling papers around. Get into the virtual classroom well enough ahead of time so that everything will be ready when participants start to log on.

Anticipating and Avoiding Problems

There are only a few things that we can count on in this life. One is that things will change. Another is that, despite our best efforts, things do not always go the way that we expect them to go. People drop out at the last minute—or don't show up. The reservations for the training room, equipment, or refreshments are lost. The room is set up classroom style when you asked for round tables in a semicircle. The participant workbooks are missing pages. Materials you shipped to the training site did not arrive. The projector isn't compatible with your laptop. The video didn't arrive or the DVD player doesn't work. The software turns out to have too many technical glitches to be functional. Participants in a virtual workshop can't log on.

It's impossible to anticipate every problem. But you can take steps to avoid certain problems and handle others if they do come up. Here are a few suggestions:

- *Think about what could go wrong and prepare backup plans.* Having a list of possible problems with steps to take if any of them occur goes a long way toward helping you relax and deal with whatever does come up.
- *Confirm and reconfirm everything.* Avoid scheduling foul-ups by double- and triple-checking the room and equipment reservations, the room setup request, and the refreshment order. If possible, ask that the room be set up the day before so you can check it yourself and make sure the equipment is working.
- *Send reminders.* Make sure that participants know to get in touch with you right away if they can't be there. Ask managers to keep you informed about issues that might mean pulling people out of training.
- *Carry spare parts.* Projector bulbs burn out, so keep a spare in your basic supplies box. Facilities sometimes forget to provide the cable you need to connect your laptop to the projector, or the cable might not be compatible with your computer, so carry a cable with you. Extra extension cords give you more flexibility in where you place equipment.
- *Find out who can help if there's a problem.* Make sure you have the names and telephone numbers of people who can help if the room is too hot, too cold, or not set up properly, get you an extra flip-chart easel or pad, find some writing tablets or marking pens if yours haven't arrived, and fix malfunctioning equipment.
- *Carry a master copy of the participant materials.* The only thing worse than not having the participant materials arrive is not having anything from which to make copies. A printout of the handouts or the handout file on a flash drive can save you a lot of grief.
- *Carry a flash drive with your PowerPoint presentation.* If you end up having to use another laptop because yours malfunctions or is not compatible with the equipment, you'll need to be able to load your presentation quickly.

Quick Review

List the three to five key learning points from this chapter that will be most helpful to you.

_____

_____

_____

_____

_____

What's Next?

In the first five chapters of this book you have learned about the tasks involved in scheduling and preparing for a workshop that provide a foundation for a successful workshop. In the next chapters, you'll learn strategies for delivering the workshop in a way that helps the participants learn and achieves the desired outcomes.

Apply What You Learn

1. Create a checklist of things you need to do to prepare for your workshop.
2. Use the suggestions in this chapter to practice delivering your workshop. If possible, use the feedback form on page 107 to obtain feedback on your delivery from some colleagues.

Answers to Exercise

Check What You Know

Which of the statements about presentation fear, or "stage fright" are accurate?

1. _X_ Symptoms of anxiety and nervousness are a natural human reaction to stress.
2. ___ For nearly everyone, the symptoms of "stage fright" disappear with sufficient experience.
3. ___ The most effective way to prevent or reduce anxiety and nervousness is to memorize the workshop script, word for word.
4. _X_ Establishing rapport with the participants can help to reduce symptoms of nervousness.
5. _X_ Being well prepared makes you less prone to symptoms of nervousness because it increases your sense of confidence.

Feedback Form

Please observe my delivery and give me feedback on how well I did the following:

❑ Appeared confident and knowledgeable

_____

_____

❑ Established and maintained rapport with participants

_____

_____

❑ Presented a professional appearance

_____

_____

❑ Delivered material clearly

_____

_____

❑ Used visual aids and media well

_____

_____

❑ Listened and responded to participants

_____

_____

❑ Spoke clearly and loudly enough to be heard

_____

_____

❑ Set the right pace and tone

_____

_____

❑ Managed the group well

_____

_____

❑ Other comments

_____

_____

_____

_____

6

Getting Started

Check What You Know

Cybelle has worked hard to plan and prepare for her meeting planning workshop. As Leon advised, she spent enough time practicing so that she felt confident she could deliver the material effectively. She decided what to wear, got everything ready, and went to bed early the night before so she would be rested and relaxed.

   Now the day of the workshop has arrived. What are some things that Cybelle can do to make sure that she starts the workshop in a way that sets a positive tone for the day?

_____

_____

_____

_____

_____

When we met with a real estate agent to discuss the sale of the home in which we had raised our kids, the first thing he said was, "We've got to get this place cleaned up."

"What's wrong with it?" my husband and I asked. "It's a pretty comfortable house."

"Sure, it is, I agree," the realtor said. "But I have to look at it through the eyes of a prospective buyer. And from that point of view . . . ."

Suddenly we became aware of the overstuffed bookshelves that lined the living room, the fraying carpet, the sofa that was already old when we bought it. We saw the kitchen wall that still bore our kids' drawings, our daughter's neon-pink bedroom (her color choice), and all the other things that made the house a home for us but would make it appear shabby and cluttered to a prospective buyer.

At the urging of the realtor, we hired a stager, an amazing woman who in the space of a few short weeks transformed our comfy home into a place that looked as if it belonged on a magazine cover. Neighbors who came to the first open house kept shaking their heads, saying, "I'd never have believed it." And soon we had an offer from a young couple who fell in love with the house the moment they walked in the door.

You'll never have to tell me again—first impressions count.

What's in this chapter will help you apply that lesson to the way you deliver your training workshops. You'll learn:

- How to get started on the right foot
- What to do before the participants arrive
- How to make people feel welcome
- How to open the workshop

> *We already have the authority; standing in front of a group naturally grants us a certain position. Now our challenge lies in winning the trust and respect of others.*

Terrence L. Gargiulo, "Incredible Credibility," in T.L. Gargiulo, A.J. Pangarkar, and T. Kirkwood (Eds.), *The Trainer's Portable Mentor*

1. Getting Off on the Right Foot

Check What You Know

Here is a description of the first few minutes of a workshop. What would be your first impressions of this trainer and of how the day is likely to go? Why?

You arrive at 8:55. The workshop is scheduled to begin at 9:00. The trainer, Daniel, is busy cuing up a DVD and testing the monitor. The room is set up classroom style, with long tables set out in rows facing the presentation area. You find an empty seat and nod hellos to a few people you recognize. Daniel walks quickly to the back of the room, strips tape off a box, and piles workbooks on a table. More people arrive. It is now 9:05. Daniel glances at the clock and says, "We'll get started in a minute." He turns his back to the group, writes "Please come back on time from the break" on a flip-chart page, and carries the page across the room, where he posts it near the door. You take out your phone and check your e-mail. Daniel turns on the slide projector and the words "Welcome" appear on the screen in fuzzy letters. Daniel mutters something under his breath and adjusts the focus. Then he turns to the group as if has seen them for the first time and asks them to help him rearrange the tables.

Your impressions of the trainer? Of how the day is likely to go?

_____

_____

_____

_____

_____

_____

What people see when they walk into the training room and what happens during the first few minutes of the workshop sets the tone for the entire session. From the moment participants arrive, they're looking for cues about what the workshop will be like—Formal or informal? Serious or fun? Interesting or dull? Risky or safe? They're making judgments about the trainer—Organized and in charge? Friendly and competent? Trustworthy? Those first impressions can have real effects on the success of the training. In fact, negative first impressions can color the participants' entire experience, and they can be difficult to change.

Workshops like Daniel's, where people arrive to find the trainer rushing around taping down electric cords, unpacking boxes, moving furniture, setting up equipment, and preparing flip-chart pages may not get off to a good start. When the trainer seems so disorganized, even frantic, people are apt to get the impression that the day will be tense and difficult.

Things are more likely to go well when participants arrive to find that everything is ready to go—when they are greeted by a friendly, relaxed trainer who seems to have done nothing that day but walk into a perfectly arranged room and wants nothing more than to deliver this workshop. Unlike Daniel, that trainer conveys an impression that he or she is competent, in control, and cares about what he or she is doing.

But that kind of positive impression doesn't just happen. Getting your workshop started in a way that sets the right tone and establishes an environment that is conducive to learning is the result of deliberate actions on your part. You'll learn about those actions in this chapter. First, here's an overview:

- *Get there early.* No matter how carefully you've prepared, there will be a lot to do in the training room before participants arrive. Get started early enough so that everything will be ready when they walk into the room.

- *Make people feel welcome.* A friendly greeting goes a long way toward helping people feel comfortable with you and in the training environment.

- *Start on time.* Getting started late not only means that you'll be playing catch-up all day, but it's really not fair to people who have made it their business to arrive on time.

- *Establish rapport, trust, and credibility.* The more quickly you can connect with the learners and earn their trust and confidence, the easier it will be to engage them in the learning process.

- *Help people get to know one another.* The more at ease participants are with one another, the more likely they are to participate actively and take the risks that are part of learning.

- *Involve people right away.* An interesting, relevant, and engaging activity draws people in, stimulates their interest, and lets them know that this is a learner-centered workshop.

- *Let people know what to expect.* An overview of the objectives and agenda gives people a road map that helps them see where they are going and how they are going to get there.

- *Help people recognize the value of the training.* An activity that helps people understand why they are learning goes a long way toward engaging them and getting them ready to learn.

2. What to Do Before Participants Arrive

Check What You Know

Suppose you are about to deliver the new hire orientation workshop mentioned in the last chapter. The workshop is scheduled to start at 9:00 A.M. You made sure to get to the training room by 8:00, so you can be ready to go when participants arrive. What are some of the tasks that you need to do?

_____

_____

_____

_____

_____

One of the best pieces of advice I received as a new trainer was "Get there early!"

"When you have people over for dinner," an experienced colleague told me, "don't you want to be relaxed and ready when your guests arrive, not frantically unpacking your groceries and trying to get the meal into the oven?"

Thinking about workshop participants as my guests went a long way toward helping me understand the importance of being ready when they arrived. Just as there were always lots of things to do when I had a dinner party, there were always lots of things to do before a workshop started, so I had to arrive early if I wanted to make sure that the first impressions my "guests" had of me were of a trainer who was organized, relaxed, and in control.

To convey the positive first impression that can be so vital to the success of a workshop, plan on arriving at least an hour before the scheduled start time. Use that time for such tasks as making sure the room is set up the way you want it; checking to see that you have all the equipment you need and that it's in working order; unpacking and arranging participant materials and supplies; and posting prepared flip-chart pages. That extra time also gives you a chance to make yourself comfortable in the room before people start streaming in.

Do You Need Extra Chairs?

It's a good idea to have a few extra chairs in the training room in case you need them. But sometimes the facilities people put too many chairs around the tables. When that happens, I remove the extras and put them at the back of the room so people won't sit on them. That's because I want to be sure that each table ends up with the right number of participants, instead of having four people at one table and seven at another. If there are no extra chairs in the room, I usually go out and find some, just in case they're needed.

Check the Seating

Even if you've been careful to provide the facilities people with a seating diagram and confirmed the arrangements carefully, you might still find that the room has been set up incorrectly. I've arrived more than once to find that the tables had been set up in rows, classroom style, when I clearly requested a chevron configuration. As you learned earlier in this book, the seating arrangement can have significant effects on the learning environment, so if it's not what you want, find someone who can help you rearrange it, or do it yourself.

As you check the seating arrangement, and make any necessary changes, also check the sightlines. Are there any posts in the room that might block people's vision? Are any seats so close to the screen that people would have to crane their necks? Too far to the sides or the back of the room for people to see the flip charts easily? Make sure that every participant, including those at the sides and toward the back, will be able to see you, the flip charts, the screen, and the monitor without twisting around. If not, make the necessary adjustments.

Check the Equipment

Make sure that all the equipment you need is in the room and in working order. Here are some things to look for:

> **A Tape Trick**
>
> Before the workshop starts, tear off pieces of the masking tape or painter's tape you'll be using to post flip-chart pages on the wall. Stick the pieces of tape to the backs of the easels so they will be out of sight but right at hand when you need them.

- *Flip-chart easels.* Do you have the right number of easels? Are any of them unstable? Is there enough paper left on the pads? Do you have extra pads in case you need them? If the facility has provided marking pens and whiteboard markers, make sure they have enough ink. Otherwise, put them aside or throw them away and use your own.

- *Slide projector and screen.* Has the screen been pulled down or set up? Is the projector working and the right distance from the screen? Do you have the right cables to connect your laptop to the projector? Set everything up and test it. Make sure that the electric cords are taped down so that you do not trip on them.

- *DVD player and monitor.* If you will be showing any DVDs, is the DVD player hooked up to the monitor? Are they both plugged in and in working order? Is the monitor in a position—or can it be easily moved to a position—where everyone can see it? Cue up your DVD and test it.

- *CD or iPod.* Set up any CD or audio files you will be using, check the volume, and make sure the audio is ready to turn on when you need it.

- *Computers.* Are any computers you will be using in the room and ready to go? Has the right software been loaded? Turn on the computers—and the monitors—and make sure that they are ready to go.

- *Microphone.* If you are using a microphone, set it up, test it to make sure it's working, and practice using it as you move around the room. Make sure you know how to turn it off.

Prepare the Presentation Area, Materials and Supplies

Set up your presentation area so that you can easily get to your trainer guide and notes without bumping into or tripping over anything. If there's a podium you do not plan to use, move it out of the way.

Put the participant workbooks or handouts folders on the tables, along with name tents, writing tablets, and pencils or pens. Leave a couple of marking pens on each table for the name tents. Neatly arrange any handouts, materials, and supplies that you won't use until later in the workshop on a table at the back or on the side of the room, where they will be accessible but not obtrusive. If people need to sign a participant roster, tape it to a table near the door or the refreshment table and put out some pens. I usually put a sign on the wall that says, "Please sign here," with an arrow pointing down toward the roster.

If you have brought prepared flip-chart pages or posters, post them before participants arrive. Tape down the bottoms of the pages so they do not flop around. The less time you need to take during the workshop to post things, the better.

Should You Conceal Prepared Flip-Chart Pages?

Some trainers prefer not to post prepared flip-chart pages until they are ready to use them, not wanting to reveal the information too early. I never do that myself—I don't mind if people see something they will not understand until later. But if you do want to conceal what's written on a prepared flip-chart page, you can still post it before the workshop starts—just tape up the bottom half. Then you can release the tape and dramatically reveal the page when you're ready.

Make Sure That Refreshments Arrive

One reason to provide refreshments is to help people feel welcome and settle in more comfortably. When you order refreshments, ask that they be delivered fifteen or twenty minutes before the workshop is scheduled to start. If they haven't arrived by that time, check on them right away. It's distracting when someone wheels a cart full of refreshments into the room while the workshop is just getting underway.

If possible, have the refreshments set up on a table at the back of the room so that people can get up and refill their cups and plates as unobtrusively as possible.

Make Yourself at Home in the Space

You can reduce nervous symptoms and get the workshop started more smoothly if you already feel comfortable in the training room. Take a few minutes after you've set everything up to walk around the room and get a sense of what it feels like being in the space. Stand in the presentation area, imagine the participants in their seats, and deliver the first few words of the opening loudly enough to reach the people at the back tables. Run through the first few slides and decide where to stand when you show them. Walk around the tables as if you were monitoring the group while they work on an activity. The more at ease you feel in the space, the more relaxed you will feel and the more confidence you will project.

Before Participants Arrive

- Check the seating arrangements and make any necessary adjustments.
- Check the equipment to make sure it's working.
- Prepare the trainer area.
- Check the sightlines.
- Arrange the materials and supplies.
- Post prepared flip-chart pages and posters.
- Make sure that refreshments arrive and are set up where you want them.
- Make yourself at home in the space.

3. Greet People and Make Them Feel Welcome

THINK ABOUT IT

When you think back to the workshops you've attended, what did the trainers do when you arrived to make you feel welcome?

_____

_____

_____

_____

People often come to training with some trepidation—that slightly unsettled feeling that many of us had on the first day of school, in a different classroom with a new teacher and kids we didn't know. A friendly, welcoming teacher probably helped us feel more comfortable and settle in more quickly. In the same way, a polite, friendly, personal greeting from a trainer goes a long way toward helping workshop participants feel comfortable and establishing a positive expectation of what is to come.

Try to finish your setup tasks at least ten minutes before the workshop is scheduled to begin so you can be ready to greet participants as they come into the room. You can stand by the door as they arrive or move around the room to introduce yourself. A handshake, a friendly smile, and a few words of greeting—"Hi, I'm Lily. It's nice to meet you"—is all you need. You can also help people settle in by helping them find seats introducing them to other participants, and encouraging them to help themselves to refreshments. The point is to make everyone feel welcome.

If people arrive early, while you are still busy checking equipment or arranging the materials, pause in your work to greet them before continuing with your setup. You might also want to have something ready for early arrivals to do—something for them to read or a question for them to ponder.

When People Arrive Early

Just as there are usually people who arrive after a workshop has started, there are often some people who arrive early. Giving them something to do while you are completing the preparations can help them focus on the workshop instead of on checking their messages. Here are some suggestions:

- Make sure that refreshments are there well ahead of the scheduled start time so that you can offer early arrivals something to eat and drink.
- Put something interesting for people to read out on the tables.
- Suggest that early arrivals read the supplementary information in the participant workbook.
- Give early arrivals the option of completing a brief activity, such as a crossword puzzle or a questionnaire that is related to the topic.
- Ask early arrivals to make a list of questions that they would like answered during the workshop.
- Post flip-chart pages with interesting, relevant quotes or questions around the room.
- If participants do not know one another well, suggest that they talk with other early arrivals about themselves and their reasons for attending the workshop.

Check What You Know

Why is it important to start a workshop on time? What are some ways you can think of for getting started on time?

_____

_____

_____

_____

_____

_____

Start on Time

Starting a workshop late not only means that you'll have less time to get through all the items on the agenda, but it's not fair to make those participants who do arrive on time sit around and wait. Unfortunately, the reality is that trainers often have to struggle with the challenge of a room that is still half-empty when the start time rolls around. No trainer I know has ever found a solution that works every time, but these strategies can help:

- *Send e-mail reminders.* Even when it's on a calendar, people may be so busy that they forget about the workshop. Send out a reminder a day or two ahead of time. Include the date, location, and start time, just in case. Ask people to reply to the message so that you know they've received it and to get in touch with you right away if they will be late or won't be able to attend. Call or e-mail anyone who doesn't respond to the message.

- *Send a text reminder.* Make sure that you have everyone's cell phone number and send a text message that people receive first thing in the morning on the day of the workshop. Include the workshop title and the start time.

- *Enlist the help of participants' managers.* People are sometimes late to workshops because they think they have to finish something beforehand or they worry that they'll miss something important while they're away from their work. Encourage managers to let participants know that they consider the training important and expect them to be away on the day of the workshop.

- *Plan something interesting and relevant for the opening.* People often come late to movies because they have learned to expect twenty minutes of previews and advertising before the main event. In the same way, the participants' previous experiences with training might lead them to think that nothing much will happen for the first twenty minutes or so of the workshop. When you first notify them about the workshop and when you send out reminders, let them know that you'll be starting off with an opening activity that they won't want to miss.

Using Music to Set the Tone

Many trainers like to establish a mood by having music playing when people arrive. Music can help set the tone and make a training room seem more inviting. Choose music carefully so that it helps to create the atmosphere you want, and be careful to respect copyrights.

---

4. Opening the Workshop

The first half-hour of any workshop sets the stage for what follows. We are judged by participants who think, "Hey, this is going to be great!" or "How do I get out of here?"

Dick Leatherman, *Training Trilogy: Conducting Needs Assessment, Designing Programs, Training Skills* (3rd ed.)

Check What You Know

Eliza and Leonardo both conduct workshops for new supervisors. Which of their openings would draw you in and help you become engaged? Why?

1. _____ After introducing herself, Eliza goes around the room and asks each person to say his or her name. She shows a slide with the workshop objectives, which she reads aloud, and then shows another with the agenda, which she also reads aloud. She explains that lunch will be served in an adjoining room at noon and asks people to turn off their cell phones. Then she briefly explains the purpose of the workshop, stressing its importance to the organization's goals. She shows slides with the company's mission and values statements, explaining that these statements should guide their actions as supervisors. She asks whether participants have questions. One participant asks whether someone will validate their parking. When no one else has questions, Eliza say, "Okay, then, let's get going," and launches into the first segment, during which she gives the group an overview of a supervisor's responsibilities.

_____

_____

(Continued)

2. _____ After introducing himself, Leonardo asks participants to introduce themselves to the other three or four people at their tables and to mention something that one of their supervisors did that helped them in their jobs. He asks someone from each table to share the best story with the group and summarizes the key actions from that story on a flip-chart page, which he posts on the wall. Then he asks the group what questions about being a supervisor they would like answered by the end of the day, writes their responses on a flip-chart page, and posts that page. He shows slides with the workshop objectives and agenda, relating them to the participants' questions. Before proceeding, he gives participants two or three minutes to think about the ways in which learning to be a better supervisor is likely to benefit them, write their responses in their workbooks, and share them with partners. Then he covers the logistics, such as parking validations and the timing of lunch and breaks, and makes a transition to the first segment, in which participants will work in small groups to discuss what a supervisor does.

_____

_____

You probably thought that the way Leonardo opened his workshop would be more likely to draw you in and engage you in the learning process. He immediately established the expectation that this would be a learner-centered workshop and used relevant, non-threatening activities that helped people get to know one another and participating actively right away.

Eliza's opening, on the other hand, might leave participants wondering why they are there and how they'll ever make it through the day. She conveyed the message that this would be a trainer-centered workshop, where she, the trainer, would do most of the talking while they, the participants, did the listening. She did nothing to help them get to know one another, to stimulate their thinking about and interest in the topic, or to help them see how the training would benefit them. By the end of the opening, they were probably still waiting for the workshop to begin and wondering why they were there.

The way you open a workshop can have a significant effect on how well people are able to learn. It's during the first few minutes that you set the tone, establish a positive learning environment, stimulate people's interest, give them a good idea about what to expect, and let them know what you expect of them. Too often, trainers like Eliza spend that valuable time talking to participants instead of engaging them in the material and the learning process.

An opening should accomplish the following:

- Help people get to know you and one another
- Stimulate participants' interest in the topic and engage them in the learning process
- Establish rapport, trust, and credibility
- Clarify expectations and objectives
- Answer participants' question, "What's in it for me?"
- Provide a preview of the session
- Address participants' concerns
- Establish ground rules
- Set up a parking lot for side issues
- Provide logistical information

Check What You Know

Describe an activity that you have used or that you have seen another trainer use that helped people in a workshop get to know one another.

_____

_____

_____

_____

Help People Get to Know You and One Another

In one of my first workshops, I was well into the opening when a participant raised her hand. "Excuse me for interrupting," she said. "But I don't know most of the people in this room. Could we take a moment to introduce ourselves?"

Some trainers launch right into the purpose and objectives of the workshop without introducing themselves or giving participants a chance to get to know the other people in the room. Start by introducing yourself. Explain your relationship to the organization and how you came to be delivering this workshop. Keep it brief and friendly. Make eye contact with individuals in the room while you speak—that's the first step in establishing rapport.

Once you've introduced yourself, do something to help participants get to know one another so that they will be more comfortable working together. Many trainers go around the room and ask the participants to introduce themselves, saying something about the jobs they do or why they are attending the workshop. I find that if there are more than ten or twelve people in the room, that kind of introduction becomes tedious, and people usually forget the names as soon as they hear them.

An alternative is to ask people to introduce themselves to the others at their tables; another is to ask them to introduce themselves to three people who are not at their table—that's a good way of getting them on their feet and mingling. Even better is an activity that combines introductions with a brief activity that starts people thinking about the subject. You can do that by posing a relevant question: "Introduce yourself to someone you do not know and share the best experience you've had as a customer"; "Introduce yourself to the people at your table and share one thing you'd like to know about writing a business plan"; or "Introduce yourself to the person next to you and share something you would like to know about closing a sale." Whatever method you use, it should help people become acquainted, put them at ease, and start them speaking up in the group and/or interacting with other participants.

Stimulate Participants' Interest in the Topic and Engage Them in the Learning Process

Good salespeople know that their first task is to get their prospects' attention and interest them in what they have to say. Otherwise, it can be useless to bother making a sales presentation. When deciding how to open a workshop, trainers can benefit from keeping the sales model in mind: the first task is to get participants' attention and interest them in the topic. Once they're interested, it will be much easier to engage them in the learning process.

Just as there are many ways to help participants get to know one another, there are many ways to stimulate their interest in the topic. One way is to ask a question that encourages people tell their own stories ("What's the best experience you had as a customer?") or come up with the reasons for doing what they will learn to do ("What are some reasons for improving the way we conduct hiring interviews?"). Another is to tell a story and ask participants to pull out the key points related to the topic.

Sometimes trainers begin by doing or showing something dramatic and surprising. For example, in a workshop for sheriffs' deputies on writing incident reports, a trainer I worked with had someone come into the room during introductions, make a loud statement, and then leave. The trainer then asked participants to describe what they had seen and heard—and pointed out the discrepancies in what they noticed and remembered.

Trainers also use games or quizzes ("Take this quiz to see what you already know about the questions you can legally ask during a hiring interview—you have three minutes") to stimulate interest and start people thinking about the topic. Whatever you use, it should be brief, relevant, engaging, and, like the sales model, capture the participants' attention and help prepare them to learn.

About Icebreakers

An icebreaker is an opening activity that is designed to help workshop participants get to know one another and feel comfortable in the training room. Many icebreakers are designed to do nothing but accomplish those two goals. But the most useful opening activities are those that also stimulate participants' interest in the subject, set the tone for the workshop, and engage people in the learning process.

There are hundreds, if not thousands, of suggestions for icebreakers and other opening activities in books and on websites related to training. Look for one that accomplishes the following:

- Gives people a chance to introduce themselves to one another
- Helps people relax and focus their attention on the workshop
- Establishes the expectation that this will be a learner-centered, not a trainer-centered workshop
- Helps people feel comfortable speaking up and participating actively
- If possible, stimulates participants' interest in what they are going to learn

Delivering Training Workshops: Pfeiffer Essential Guides to Training Basics.
Copyright © 2010 by John Wiley & Sons, Inc.
Reproduced by permission of Pfeiffer, an Imprint of Wiley. www.Pfeiffer.com

Check What You Know

Which of the following would be effective ways of establishing rapport, trust, and credibility?

1. _____ When you introduce yourself, speak clearly in a friendly, casual, but professional voice and make eye contact with participants.
2. _____ Hand out copies of your resume and explain your qualifications for conducting this workshop.
3. _____ Demonstrate your knowledge of the subject by telling participants something they do not know about it.
4. _____ Use participants' names and listen carefully to what they have to say.
5. _____ Let people know that you are aware of and respect the knowledge and experience they bring to the workshop.

Establish Rapport, Trust, and Credibility

Nervousness during the first few minutes of a workshop leads some trainers to speak rapidly and look over the participants' heads or down at their notes instead of making eye contact. But that behavior creates distance between the trainer and the participants; it also makes the trainer seem less credible. Instead, use the opening to build on the positive first impression you made by greeting people as they came into the room. Speak clearly in a friendly, casual, but professional voice, and make eye contact with individuals. Stay focused and enthusiastic—help participants feel as if there is nowhere in the world that you would rather be. Demonstrate your interest in the participants by listening carefully to their questions or responses.

Look for opportunities to let people know that you are aware of and respect the knowledge and experience they bring to the workshop. You might say something like, "From the questionnaires you sent in before the workshop, it's clear that you already know a lot about strategic planning. My job today is to help you build on that knowledge."

An important part of establishing rapport with people is to use their names. Using people's names automatically makes a personal connection. When referring to something that someone said earlier, say, "Jake, a few minutes ago you mentioned that. . . ." When responding to a question, say, "Melinda, that's a great question" or "Melinda, there are six important reasons for. . . ." Be careful, however, not to use names to single people out in ways that might put them on the spot or embarrass them: Instead of saying, "Peter, why don't you tell the group what you think about . . . ," ask the question of the group: "Who would like to tell us what you think about . . . ?

To establish rapport and trust, and to engage people in the learning process, it's important for you to convey enthusiasm. I've attended workshops in which the trainer began with some variant of, "I know we'd all rather be doing something else, but we only have four hours to get through this, so we'd better get started." How in the world, I wondered, could the trainer expect us, the participants, to be enthusiastic about the learning experience if he is so obviously dreading it?

If you want participants to be enthusiastic about learning, you have to be enthusiastic yourself. Enthusiasm

Name Tents or Name Tags?

Few trainers are able to memorize all participants' names, at least not right away, so you'll need to rely on name tags or name tents. My preference is for name tents, unless people will be on their feet and moving around a lot during the day. Name tags have a way of disappearing onto coats and jackets that end up on the backs of chairs, and if they're too small—which they usually are—you won't be able to see them from the front of the room.

Name tents, which can be made quickly from folded five-by-eight-inch cards, are usually more helpful than name tags. I ask participants to use marking pens to write their first names on both sides of the fold in large, clear letters and to keep the cards in front of them. If they change tables, I remind them to take their cards along. The disadvantage is that, unlike name tags, people do not carry their name cards around when they are on their feet.

is contagious: Witness the fans at a baseball game when their team puts out an extra effort to score a run. But enthusiasm is helpful only if it is sincere. You don't have to think that the subject is the most fascinating in the world, but you do have to be excited about helping people learn something that will be useful to them and their organization. You have to want to communicate and interact with participants and to guide them through the learning process. If so, your body language will convey that enthusiasm to the workshop participants.

Delivering Training Workshops: Pfeiffer Essential Guides to Training Basics.
Copyright © 2010 by John Wiley & Sons, Inc.
Reproduced by permission of Pfeiffer, an Imprint of Wiley. www.Pfeiffer.com

Check What You Know

Which of the following would be the most effective way to help participants clarify their expectations and objectives?

1. _____ Show the workshop objectives on a slide, point out the agenda you have posted on the wall, and ask whether anyone has questions.
2. _____ Tell participants to read the objectives in their workbooks and add any others that they might have.
3. _____ Ask participants to discuss their expectations and objectives with partners, then, ask for volunteers to share their objectives with the group.

Clarify Expectations and Objectives

During the preparation process, you will probably have had the opportunity to gather information about what participants hope to accomplish in the workshop. Let them know that you've paid attention. One way to do that is to prepare a flip-chart page with a summary of their expectations and objectives. During the opening of the workshop, review the items on the flip-chart page, and ask whether anyone has something to add. When the list is complete, be sure to address any expectations or objectives that will not be met in the workshop.

If you were not able to gather expectations and objectives ahead of time, you can use one of these methods to elicit them during the opening:

- Ask the group, "What would you like to know or be able to do by the end of this workshop?" Write everything that people come up with on a flip-chart page. Post the page and keep it up for reference during the workshop. During the closing, ask people to determine how well their expectations and objectives were met.

- Ask participants to discuss their expectations and objectives with partners or in small groups. Then go around the room and ask a few people to share what they came up with. Write their responses on a flip-chart page and post the page.

- Post several blank flip-chart pages on the wall. Ask participants to write one or two of their objectives on a flip-chart page and then give them a few minutes to look over the pages with the other participants' objectives.

Check What You Know

What's one way in which a trainer can help workshop participants discover the answer to the all-important question, "What's in it for me?"

_____

_____

_____

_____

Answer "What's in It for Me?"

As you learned earlier in this book, all workshop participants want to know how the workshop is going to benefit them, even if no one asks the question directly. In other words, they want to know, "Why am I spending time here when I could be doing something important? How is this workshop going to help me be better at my job, work more quickly and more productively, and advance in my career?"

Many trainers respond to this question by providing a list of benefits. But it's much more effective to help people discover the answer to "What's in it for me?" for themselves. One way to do that is to ask them to work on their own, in small groups, or with partners to write down all the ways in which the learning could help them do their jobs or advance in their careers and then ask volunteers to share what they wrote. You could also ask people to select a current challenge and think of ways in which what they learn in the workshop could help them address it. What's important is to make sure that participants understand the value of the training so that they will be more motivated to engage actively in the learning process.

Provide a Preview of the Workshop

Even if you've sent out the agenda ahead of time, go over it quickly before launching into the first segment. Relate the agenda items to the participants' expectations and objectives. Point out times for breaks. For multi-session workshops, briefly go over the agenda for each session. Mention that the agenda is flexible and subject to change, but that you will always stop on time for breaks and end the workshop on time (and keep that promise).

I like to put the agenda on a flip-chart page and post it where people can see it throughout the workshop. The agenda acts as a checklist for me and for the group: "We've covered the process of planning for the interview" [✓]. "Now let's move on to techniques for asking questions."

By the way, it's a good idea to leave times off any agenda that you send to participants, post in the training room, or put in the participant workbook— you might not end up following the original timetable, and people can be distracted when the times in the agenda don't match up with the actual times for different segments and activities.

Address Participants' Concerns

Workshop participants worry about everything from whether they'll be asked to do role plays to what time you plan to stop for lunch. Prepare a flip-chart page summarizing any concerns that participants mentioned before the workshop. Take a few minutes to address those concerns and any others that people may have. Do that before you move into the first segment of the workshop. You might say things like: "Some of you are concerned about having to do role-play activities. I think role plays can be very helpful, so I will ask for volunteers to do some role plays later on. But I'll only call on volunteers." "I understand that some of you have an important meeting at lunchtime, so we'll take an extra few minutes. We'll break at 11:50 and come back by 1:10." "Before we leave today, we'll discuss ways to help your managers understand why you are going to make changes in the way that you write reports."

Check What You Know

What are some examples of ground rules that can help a workshop run more smoothly?

_____

_____

_____

_____

Establish Ground Rules

Ground rules can help a workshop run more smoothly. Examples include, "Cell phones and pagers off" and "Listen while others are talking."

People are more likely to honor ground rules when they have had some say in establishing them. Explain that the purpose of ground rules is to help everyone use the workshop time to best advantage. Write one or two ground rules that you consider important on a flip-chart page and elicit others from the group. Post the page so you or the other participants can invoke ground rules if they are needed.

Establishing ground rules should be one of the last things you do during the opening. I usually do this task after reviewing the agenda but before covering logistical information (such as where to find the restrooms).

Typical ground rules include the following:

- Cell phones, pagers, and mobile devices turned off or set to vibrate.
- Listen while others are speaking.
- What we say in this room stays in this room.
- No side conversations.
- Respect differing points of view.
- Give everyone a chance to speak.
- Keep an open mind.
- Come back on time from breaks.

Set Up a Parking Lot

Side issues and questions that are not relevant to the topic at hand can derail discussions, throwing the workshop off track. A parking lot, which is a flip-chart page (or pages) on which you can post those kinds of issues and questions, helps you keep everyone's focus on the topic at hand.

Like establishing ground rules, setting up the parking lot is best done after reviewing the agenda. Label a flip-chart page "parking lot" and post it on the wall (or prepare the flip-chart page and post it before the workshop starts). Explain that when issues come up that are not immediately relevant to the current activity or discussion, or that are beyond the scope of the workshop, you will note them in the parking lot (chances are that one or more such issues have already been raised). Say that you will go through the list at the end of the workshop to make sure that everything has been addressed and decide what to do with any items that may remain. Putting items you cannot address immediately in the parking lot helps you keep discussions focused while letting people know that you consider their questions, concerns, and issues important.

Provide Logistical Information

Wrap up the opening by giving participants any logistical information they will need: where the restrooms are, how to get parking tickets validated, where lunch will be served, how to use the workbooks, the location of breakout rooms, and so on.

Also give participants a chance to ask any questions before you move on. But be careful not to become sidetracked into discussions of topics that you will be covering later in the workshop. Refer to the agenda and say something like, "Jason, we'll be discussing those issues later this morning, so please hold your questions until then." You can also write questions you are not ready to answer on a flip-chart page and post the page so that people know that they have been heard.

Opening a Virtual Workshop

The way you open a virtual workshop is just as important—possibly more important—than the way you open a live, in-person workshop. In a virtual workshop, you have only a minute or two to capture participants' attention, help them feel connected to you and the others in the "room," and engage them in the learning process. And it's much easier for participants to leave a virtual training room if they fail to become engaged.

For a positive start to your virtual workshops, consider the following:

- *Be ready to go when participants log on to the training room.* That means starting your preparation forty-five to sixty minutes ahead of time so you can set up the room, try everything out, make sure that you are comfortable, and be ready to greet people when they enter the room. As people "arrive," greet them by name and ask for a response to make sure that their audio connections are working.

- *Get started on time.* Virtual workshops are relatively short—most are sixty to ninety minutes, and rarely do they extend beyond two hours. Getting started late wastes precious time, and people who have already logged on are liable to disappear if they have to sit there and wait.

- *Start a conversation with any early arrivals.* In a live, in-person workshop, people can mingle and chat over coffee while they wait for the workshop to start. Try to create the same friendly, informal atmosphere in a virtual workshop. Ask people questions, introduce them to one another, and encourage them to share information about themselves, such as the kinds of jobs they do, their reasons for attending the workshop, something they'd like to know about the topic, and so on.

- *Do something interactive right away.* Asking a question that requires a response or asking people to do something establishes the expectation that this will be an interactive, learner-focused experience, not a presentation. It also helps people become familiar with the tools and technology and alerts you to any technical problems a participant might be having.

- *Identify the participants.* Unless the group is more than about fifteen people, put up a list with participants' names—and their companies, departments, and positions, if appropriate. Ask people to say their names so that they can hear one another's voices. If the group is small enough, you can ask people to answer a question, such as, "What's one thing you would like to accomplish today?" or "What is something you hope to learn about . . .?" Make sure that they keep their responses brief.

- *Do some opening activities.* The opening activities in a virtual workshop have the same function as in a live, in-person workshop—for example, to help people establish rapport, start them thinking about what they are going to learn, and help them recognize the benefits of the training.

For a virtual workshop, the opening activities should also give people practice using the tools, including raising their hands, asking or answering questions, and using the chat function.

- *Provide an overview of the session.* Participants in a virtual workshop need a look at the agenda so they know what will be covered. They also need to know what time the workshop will end and what kinds of activities will take place. Leave a little time for people to ask questions before you begin the first item on the agenda.

Quick Quiz

List the three to five key learning points from this chapter that will be most helpful to you.

_____

_____

_____

_____

_____

What's Next?

Training is as much about communication as anything. To be able to deliver a workshop that achieves results, a trainer needs to be able to communicate clearly and effectively. That means being able to manage the nervousness that can interfere with communication and honing the skills that make it possible to deliver training in a way that helps people learn. You'll learn how to do those things in the next chapter.

Apply What You Learn

Use the worksheet at the end of the chapter to plan an opening for your workshop.

Answers to Exercises

Check What You Know

Eliza and Leonardo both conduct workshops for new supervisors. Which of their openings would draw you in and help you become engaged? Why?

1. _____ After introducing herself, Eliza goes around the room and asks each person to say his or her name. She shows a slide with the workshop objectives, which she reads aloud, and then shows another with the agenda, which she also reads aloud. She explains that lunch will be served in an adjoining room at noon and asks people to turn off their cell phones. Then she briefly explains the purpose of the workshop, stressing its importance to the organization's goals. She shows slides with the company's mission and values statements, explaining that these statements should guide their actions as supervisors. She asks whether participants have questions. One participant asks whether someone will validate their parking. When no one else has questions, Eliza say, "Okay, then, let's get going," and launches into the first segment, during which she gives the group an overview of a supervisor's responsibilities.

(Continued)

Delivering Training Workshops: Pfeiffer Essential Guides to Training Basics.
Copyright © 2010 by John Wiley & Sons, Inc.
Reproduced by permission of Pfeiffer, an Imprint of Wiley. www.Pfeiffer.com

2.   _X_ After introducing himself, Leonardo asks participants to introduce themselves to the other three or four people at their tables and to mention something that one of their supervisors did that helped them in their jobs. He asks someone from each table to share the best story with the group and summarizes the key actions from that story on a flip-chart page, which he posts on the wall. Then he asks the group what questions about being a supervisor they would like answered by the end of the day, writes their responses on a flip-chart page, and posts that page. He shows slides with the workshop objectives and agenda, relating them to the participants' questions. Before proceeding, he gives participants two or three minutes to think about the ways in which learning to be a better supervisor is likely to benefit them, write their responses in their workbooks, and share them with a partner. Then he covers the logistics, such as parking validations and the timing of lunch and breaks, and makes a transition to the first segment, in which participants will work in small groups to discuss what a supervisor does.

> *Leonardo's opening would help draw participants in and engage them in the learning process. He established the expectation that this is a learner-centered workshop and he used activities to help people get to know one another and participate actively. But Eliza's opening might leave participants wondering why they are there and how they'll ever make it through the day. It implies that she will be doing most of the talking. She did not help them get to know one another, start thinking about the topic, or see how training will benefit them.*

Check What You Know

Which of the following would be effective ways of establishing rapport, trust, and credibility?

1. _X_ When you introduce yourself, speak clearly in a friendly, casual, but professional voice and make eye contact with participants.
2. ___ Hand out copies of your resume and explain your qualifications for conducting this workshop.
3. ___ Demonstrate your knowledge of the subject by telling participants something they do not know about it.
4. _X_ Use participants' names and listen carefully to what they have to say.
5. _X_ Let people know that you are aware of and respect the knowledge and experience they bring to the workshop.

Check What You Know

Which of the following would be the most effective way to help participants clarify their expectations and objectives?

1. ___ Show the workshop objectives on a slide, point out the agenda you have posted on the wall, and ask whether anyone has questions.
2. ___ Tell participants to read the objectives in their workbooks and add any others that they might have.
3. _X_ Ask participants to discuss their expectations and objectives with partners, then ask for volunteers to share their objectives with the group.

Worksheet

Plan Your Opening

Answer these questions to plan an opening for your workshop.

1. What will you to say when you introduce yourself to the group?
   _____
   _____

2. What will you do to help people get to know one another?
   _____
   _____

3. What will you do to engage participants and stimulate their interest in the subject?
   _____
   _____

4. What will you do to clarify expectations and objectives?
   _____
   _____

5. What will you do to help people see what's in it for them?
   _____
   _____

6. What ground rules would you like the group to establish?
   _____
   _____

7. What else will you do to establish an environment that is conducive to learning?
   _____
   _____

7

Delivery Skills

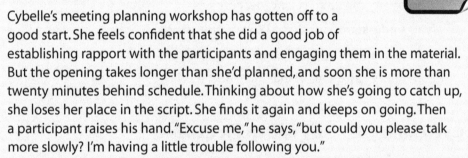

Check What You Know

Cybelle's meeting planning workshop has gotten off to a good start. She feels confident that she did a good job of establishing rapport with the participants and engaging them in the material. But the opening takes longer than she'd planned, and soon she is more than twenty minutes behind schedule. Thinking about how she's going to catch up, she loses her place in the script. She finds it again and keeps on going. Then a participant raises his hand. "Excuse me," he says, "but could you please talk more slowly? I'm having a little trouble following you."

Cybelle thanks the participant and deliberately slows her speech down. But she suddenly finds that her mouth is dry and her hands are shaking. It takes all her concentration just to keep on going.

Why did Cybelle, who was feeling so confident, suddenly experience the symptoms of nervousness? What could she have done to prevent or control them?

_____

_____

_____

I loved going to my children's school plays. All the kids—especially mine, of course—were so cute, and so much fun to watch. But it was the children I enjoyed watching, not the play. They stumbled over their lines, dropped the props, turned their backs to the audience, spoke in quivering voices and monotones. But they tried so hard, and who cared about hearing the lines; we parents were there to watch *them*.

But as an adult, I don't spend good money to watch actors fumble with their props, forget their lines, turn their backs, or speak in a monotone. I go to a play because I want the performance to delight, fascinate, frighten, or enlighten me. For that to happen, the actors need to bring the play to life, and we in the audience need to be able to see and hear them. In fact, that's one of your most important challenges as a trainer—bringing a workshop to life by presenting it clearly, confidently, and with enthusiasm to your audience.

What this chapter will help you learn:

- How to overcome anxiety and nervousness

- How to understand nonverbal communication

- How to speak so you can be heard and understood

- How to use equipment, visual aids, and media

1. Overcoming Anxiety and Nervousness

> *Anxiety comes from fear—fear of not having the answers or of being seen as incompetent. Of course, we recognize intellectually that we really don't need all the answers, but it is hard not to be concerned. . . . It's okay. We are human.*

Dick Leatherman, *Training Trilogy: Conducting Needs Assessment, Designing Programs, Training Skills* (3rd ed.)

THINK ABOUT IT

Have you experienced the symptoms of anxiety or nervousness when making a presentation, leading a meeting, delivering a workshop, or in another situation where you had to stand up and speak before a group? What were those symptoms? Why do you think you experienced them? What did you do to control them?

_____

_____

_____

_____

_____

_____

Many trainers—most of us, in fact—experience a certain amount of anxiety and nervousness when we deliver a workshop. As mentioned in Chapter 5, nearly half of the population is more afraid of speaking before a group than of standing on the edge of a precipice.

You already know that careful planning and practice can help reduce the fear. But no matter how well prepared you are and how much experience you have, the symptoms of anxiety and nervousness can strike without warning. You seem to feel relaxed and confident while you greet the participants, and then you stand up to deliver the opening and your mouth feels as if it's stuffed with cotton, your legs become jelly, your hands shake as if you were standing in a snow bank, your voice quivers like a bad recording, and the faces in the audience are a blur. You can't remember what you were doing, or what you are supposed to do next.

Those symptoms are natural human responses to stress. You can't avoid them or make them disappear just by thinking about them, but it can help to understand why you experience them. Following are some of the reasons.

- *You aren't as well prepared as you thought you were*. Perhaps instead of really practicing the workshop, all you did was read it through a few times. Becoming proficient at driving a car takes more than watching someone drive or thinking about driving; it takes *doing* it, over and over, until you become good at it. That's what practicing is all about.

- *You don't know enough about the subject*. Any uncertainty you feel about your grasp of the subject matter may result in the self-doubt that can undermine confidence. Identifying the questions that participants are likely to ask and then deciding how you would answer them can help. So can having reference material ready in case people ask questions you are not able to answer.

- *You haven't much experience standing up in front of a group*. It's normal for people to experience much more anxiety and nervousness the first few times they make a presentation or deliver a workshop than after they've done it many times. Although your nervousness might never disappear entirely, you'll not only have less of it with experience, you'll have developed ways to cope.

- *The stakes are unusually high*. You might have no difficulty delivering training in ordinary situations to people with whom you feel comfortable. But if your manager is there to review your performance, or the audience is made up of important customers or senior executives, you may feel anxious and nervous because you are worried that you'll make mistakes or appear foolish. That's why it's so important to think about the audience ahead of time, recognize when it's a high-stakes situation, and visualize the audience while you practice.

- *You are unusually tired or not feeling well*. Exhaustion or illness can make you feel less clear-headed than usual, which in turn can affect your self-confidence. Taking care of yourself should be first priority if you want to have the stamina to deliver training with confidence and enthusiasm.

Reasons for Nervousness and Anxiety

- You aren't as well prepared as you thought you were.
- You think that you don't know enough about the subject.
- You haven't much experience standing up in front of a group.
- The stakes are unusually high.
- You are unusually tired or not feeling well.

Even though feelings of anxiety and nervousness are natural, it's important to know how to reduce and control the symptoms so they don't end up derailing your workshop. Here are some strategies you might find helpful:

- *Pay special attention to the way that you prepare and practice when you feel that it is particularly important that the workshop go well.* In a high-stakes situation, you might want to make an extra effort to connect with participants ahead of time. That connection can help you feel confident that you have clarified their expectations, that they understand the purpose of the workshop, and that you are aware of any concerns they may have about the training. You might also want to make an extra effort to practice by delivering key parts of the presentation to some colleagues who play the role of the intended audience.

- *Learn enough about the subject so that you can feel confident answering participants' questions.* As mentioned earlier, you don't need to be an expert in the subject matter to deliver a great workshop. But you do need to know enough so that you don't worry about your credibility being attacked. It can help to talk the workshop through with someone who does know a lot about the subject—that person can either reassure you that your level of knowledge is fine or help fill in the missing pieces.

- *Think about what could go wrong and make backup plans.* Nervous symptoms can be triggered by last-minute logistical problems such as room mix-ups or missing or malfunctioning equipment. Worrying about what can go wrong and rushing around at the last minute trying to fix things not only distracts your focus, but it can sap the energy you need to establish rapport with the participants and engage them in the learning process. Make a list of things that could possibly go wrong and decide how you will handle each one if it does occur. Be ready with substitutes in case something you need for an activity isn't there or doesn't function properly, or if you need to save time because there was a fire drill or a discussion went on too long.

- *Take care of yourself.* Preparing for and delivering a workshop takes energy, and you need to feel at your best to be at your best. So that you can focus your attention during the workshop and bring energy and enthusiasm to the training room, make it a habit to eat well, get enough sleep and exercise, and take time for activities that help you relax.

- *Make the training room your own.* When you stay overnight in a strange hotel room, you might feel a little tentative at first. To feel comfortable, you need to know how to change the temperature and open or close the drapes, where to find the ice machine and the television remote, how to get to the bathroom in the middle of the night without tripping over something. That same tentativeness in a new training environment can appear to be a lack of self-confidence, so take whatever time you need to get to know the training room before the participants arrive.

Be ready to greet people as they arrive. When you stand up to open the workshop, you'll find that you'll feel much less nervous if you have already made a friendly contact with everyone, or nearly everyone, in the group. Greeting people when they arrive will help you see participants as individuals, rather than as a scary faceless mass.

Make eye contact with a few participants before you begin to speak. Starting to speak the moment you stand up is likely to bring on a rush of nervous symptoms. Before launching into the opening, make eye contact with a few people, then continue to connect with various individuals in the audience as you speak.

Move about. Nervousness causes some trainers to lock themselves into a rigid body posture, with their knees locked and their feet rooted to the floor. If you notice that you are fixed to one spot, move. Take a few steps toward the participants or from side to side. Don't wander or pace, just move naturally.

Avoid speeding up your speech, and respect the value of silence. Nervous trainers often begin speaking more and more rapidly, as if to get it over with as quickly as possible, and they leap into every silence. If you find yourself speeding up, slow down. Use silence to help you collect your thoughts, let participants think about how to respond to a question, and give people a chance to process what they hear.

If nervous symptoms don't subside, consider acknowledging your nervousness. This is a controversial suggestion—trainers and presenters disagree on whether it's okay to tell an audience that they are feeling nervous. But people notice the more obvious symptoms—shaking hands and voice, fumbling with equipment and papers, a frantic look on the trainer's face—and I've found that they can become uncomfortable when those symptoms continue. If you cannot get your nervous symptoms under control, it can help to take a deep breath, make eye contact with a few friendly people in the audience, and acknowledge what you are feeling: "I'm sorry, but I seem to be feeling a little nervous up here." Take another deep breath, smile, make eye contact with a few people, and then, when you feel ready, continue.

To Reduce and Control Symptoms of Anxiety and Nervousness

- Pay special attention to preparation and practice in high-stakes situations.
- Learn enough about the subject so that you can feel confident answering participants' questions.
- Think about what could go wrong and make backup plans.
- Take care of yourself.
- Make the training room your own.
- Be ready to greet people as they arrive.
- Make eye contact with a few participants before you begin to speak.
- Move about.
- Avoid speeding up your speech, and respect the value of silence.
- If necessary, consider acknowledging your nervousness.

Relaxation Techniques

To relieve the symptoms of stress, nervousness, and anxiety before and during a workshop, try these simple techniques.

- *Breathe.* Shallow, rapid breathing is a common symptom of presentation anxiety. If you become aware that you are not breathing normally, stop what you are doing—you need to get your breathing under control before you do anything else. Take a deep breath in through your nose. Then let the air out through your mouth, letting the anxiety flow out with it. Then just wait and trust your body to take a breath on its own. Don't hold your breath; just let your body take in a breath when it's ready. Repeat the process several times, until you are breathing normally again.
- *Yawn.* Yawning is a great way to relax before a workshop begins or during a break. Yawning not only helps to release tense jaws and relax your facial muscles, but it increases the saliva in your mouth, which is helpful if your mouth is dry.
- *Learn to release tension as it occurs.* When people are anxious, they often tense muscles in various parts of their body—they tighten their shoulders, clench their fists, lock their knees, freeze their facial muscles into a mask. Learn to pay attention to your body during your everyday activities. When you sense that a muscle has become tense and rigid, take a breath and let the tension go with the outgoing breath. As you increase your everyday sensitivity to tension, you'll be better able to release tense muscles when you are under stress.

Delivering Training Workshops: Pfeiffer Essential Guides to Training Basics.
Copyright © 2010 by John Wiley & Sons, Inc.
Reproduced by permission of Pfeiffer, an Imprint of Wiley. www.Pfeiffer.com

2. Understanding Nonverbal Communication

Check What You Know

Which trainer appears confident and enthusiastic about the workshop? Which do not? How can you tell?

Trainer 1

☐ Confident and enthusiastic

_____

_____

_____

_____

_____

Trainer 2

☐ Confident and enthusiastic

_____

_____

_____

_____

_____

Trainer 3

❑ Confident and enthusiastic

_____

_____

_____

_____

_____

The words we speak are only one of the ways by which we communicate. Even when we say nothing at all, someone else can tell just by looking at us whether we are feeling delighted or dismayed, energetic or tired, confident or uncertain. That's because a significant part of our communication is through our body language: posture, movement, facial expressions, and gestures. According to Carol Kinsey Goman, author of *The Nonverbal Advantage: Secrets and Science of Body Language at Work*, "Human beings are genetically programmed to look for facial and behavioral cues and to quickly understand their meaning. We see someone gesture and automatically make a judgment about the intention of that gesture."

Your facial expressions, body language, and gestures can reinforce what you say and convey sincerity, or they can conflict with your words, sending the message that you shouldn't be taken seriously—that you don't really mean what you say. Body language such as making eye contact and nodding your head while someone is speaking shows that you are interested and helps you hold the participants' attention. On the other hand, fidgeting, repetitive gestures, excessive movement, or facial tics can make you appear uncertain and be annoying and distracting.

Here are some things to consider about the use of body language:

- *Posture*. To convey energy and self-confidence, stand up straight, with your weight balanced evenly on both feet, your head up, and your shoulders oriented toward the participants. Let your arms hang loosely from your shoulders, and keep your body—especially your shoulders—relaxed, not rigid. Avoid slumping, which makes you seem unenthusiastic; crossing your arms stiffly over your chest, which can make you seem judgmental and forbidding; holding your arms stiffly at your side, which can make you seem tense; standing with your hands on your hips, which conveys impatience; or holding your hands crossed behind your back, which makes you seem uncomfortable.

- *Movement*. Avoid planting your feet into the floor as if they were growing roots—a little movement helps keep your body relaxed. But when you move, move deliberately from one point to another. It's distracting to watch a trainer shift continually from one foot to another, pace forward and back, shuffle from side to side, or do little dance steps. Instead, take a few steps toward someone who is speaking; move to one side of the room for part of a discussion, then to the other side for the next part, then back to your presentation space to signal a shift of topic.

- *Facial expression*. Even as infants, we "read" people's faces. A mother's facial expression can tell a baby whether Mommy is happy, pleased, sad, or angry. As adults, we use our understanding of facial expression to decide whether to trust people and believe what they say, to figure out how they feel about us, and to decide how to respond to them. We can become uncomfortable or suspicious when someone greets us with a forced, fixed smile, no matter how welcoming their words. We distrust someone who agrees to do us a favor when we see a flash of annoyance in his or her eyes.

  To avoid disconnects between your facial expressions and your words, be as honest, open, and sincere as possible when interacting with workshop participants. That doesn't mean that you need to say everything that you are thinking and feeling; it does mean that you need to be truthful and say that you disagree with something or are unsure about something when that is the case. It means being aware of your own feelings and avoiding expressions that convey annoyance, boredom, or impatience when people are speaking. It also means becoming aware of habitual facial expressions, such as raising your eyebrows or pursing your lips, that participants might misinterpret to mean that you are skeptical or annoyed.

Making frequent eye contact with participants, both when you are speaking and when they are speaking, is one of the best ways to ensure that your facial expressions convey enthusiasm, interest, friendliness, warmth, and caring. But when you are speaking, be sure to avoid staring at one person, making eye contact with the same person over and over again, or directing your gaze to the air above people's heads. And when you are listening, *really* listen. Even if your eyes are fixed on the person's face, your expression will quickly tell everyone if you are busy preparing a rebuttal, wishing the person would stop talking, or upset by what you are hearing.

Gesture. To a greater or lesser degree, most of us use gestures to punctuate our speech, especially to emphasize points, but also to convey feelings without words. For example, in most cultures—but not all—a shrug conveys the message, "So what," and a hand lifted with palm facing out communicates, "Stop." But some people tend to overuse gesture when they become nervous or to use habitual gestures that are distracting rather than helpful.

Try to keep your gestures natural and to a minimum. That will be easier to do if you keep your shoulders relaxed and let your arms hang loosely at your sides, as suggested above. Avoid waving your hands around or using a marking pen to punctuate your points, which can be distracting; waving or pointing your index finger, which immediately turns you into everyone's third-grade teacher; fiddling with your hair, the buttons on your shirt, or pieces of jewelry, which makes you appear nervous; touching your face, which makes you seem uncertain; clasping and unclasping your hands, which conveys a sense of desperation; or scratching, which can make everyone want to do the same.

Obtaining Feedback

It can be very challenging to become aware of your body language. Most of us can't do it alone. We need feedback from other people who can tell us when we are slumping, or looking up at the ceiling instead of at the participants, touching our fingertips to our lips while someone is speaking, waving our hands around or holding our arms too stiffly at our sides, or moving around in a distracting way.

The best feedback is seeing yourself in action. Ask someone to videotape you while you delivering a workshop or practicing your delivery so you can see your own body language from the participants' point of view. Once you have identified what you need to change, address only one or two issues at a time. If you find that you are fidgeting too much, concentrate on fidgeting less. If you are slumping, concentrate on finding a relaxed, comfortable upright posture.

To Use Positive Body Language

- Stand up straight, balance your weight evenly on both feet, keep your head up, and let your arms hang loosely from your shoulders.
- Avoid planting your feet into the floor and avoid shuffling or pacing.
- Be aware of your own feelings so you can avoid facial expressions that convey annoyance, boredom, or impatience when people are speaking.
- Make frequent eye contact with participants.
- When you are listening, *really* listen.
- Keep your gestures natural and to a minimum.

Sitting Versus Standing

Standing in front of the group implies that you are in charge and makes it easier for learners to focus on you. Sitting makes you part of the group and makes it easier for participants to focus on one another. I usually stand while I am presenting material, explaining something, and giving instructions. I also stand while I am facilitating a large-group discussion. But I often sit on a stool, lean back on the edge of a table, or sit in a chair when the participants are engaged in a discussion with one another, and I sit or stand off to the side during role plays or when a participant is presenting material to the group.

Different Cultures, Different Meanings

To avoid misunderstandings and keep from making people uncomfortable, trainers need to be aware that some body language, facial expressions, and gestures don't necessarily convey the same things to people in other cultures. For example, people in different cultures may use different gestures to wave hello or goodbye. In many places, people shake their heads up and down to indicate "yes" and side-to-side to indicate "no," while in others, it's the reverse. A gesture that communicates "come here" may mean "no" in one culture and be an insult in another. Touching someone on the shoulder as you speak might be interpreted as approval by some people and be offensive to others. People in some cultures are more comfortable standing close to others while they speak. In many cultures, people use eye contact to establish rapport and show that they are paying attention, but in others, holding eye contact with another person is considered rude.

3. Speaking So You Can Be Heard and Understood

For people to respond to what you say they must understand what you say. . . . The object is not to overwhelm people with the extent of your vocabulary but to convey a message as effectively as possible.

David Leigh, *The Group Trainer's Handbook: Designing and Delivering Training for Groups* (3rd ed.)

Check What You Know

Which of the following statements would you agree with?

1. _____ For people who have a natural tendency to speak softly, raising their voices above the level of normal speech may feel like shouting.
2. _____ The most common tendency among trainers is to speak too slowly.
3. _____ People who are not used to speaking in public often speak in a monotone.
4. _____ Using formal language, complicated words, jargon, and technical terminology helps trainers appear more educated and credible.
5. _____ The casual pronunciation we use in everyday speech, such as "hafta" instead of "have to," can seem sloppy in a workshop.

As a trainer, two of your most important tools are your voice and your words, and to communicate clearly to your audience, you need to use them well. That means speaking loudly enough so that your voice carries to the people at the back of the room, at a pace that lets people follow what you say but does not put them to sleep; using a conversational tone that communicates the meaning, not just the words; choosing words that participants can easily understand; and pronouncing those words clearly and distinctly.

Let's look more closely at those ways of making sure that you can be heard and understood.

- *Volume.* Some lucky trainers have voices that naturally "carry" or project easily over a distance. But many others, especially women, have a tendency to speak softly, and speaking more loudly than normal may feel to them like shouting. Find out how well your voice carries. If you have trouble projecting to the back row of a training room, practice until you can crank up the volume and feel comfortable with that increased volume.

- *Pace.* Some of us naturally speak quickly, others more slowly. At the extreme ends of the spectrum are people who speak so rapidly that they are impossible to understand and those who speak so slowly that you can't wait for them to get to the end of a sentence. For trainers, the most common problem is a tendency to speak too quickly, running words and sentences together without taking a breath, especially if they are nervous or think they are running out of time. For workshop participants to be able to understand you, it's important to adjust your pace so that they can easily follow what you say.

Tone. Just as we differ in the pacing of our speech, we also differ in tone. Some of us naturally vary our tone a great deal, while the speech of others is flatter, with less variation. (In fact, you can often tell where in the country someone comes from by the tone of his or her speech.) People who are unused to public speaking sometimes flatten their voices into a monotone, which can be boring to listen to and strip the meaning out of the words. Try for a conversational tone in which the pitch of your voice changes naturally to hold interest, emphasize points, and signal moves from one point to another.

Word choice. Your choice of words affects the clarity of the information you convey as well as how listeners perceive what you say. Some trainers, especially those who are proficient in the subject they are teaching, use jargon or highly technical language without stopping to consider whether participants will understand that terminology.

To Speak So You Can Be Heard and Understood

- Speak loudly enough to be heard in the back row.
- Adjust your pace so people can follow what you say.
- Use a conversational tone.
- Use simple, everyday language.
- use standard pronunciation and speak distinctly.

Watch Your Language

Language that some participants might find offensive creates discomfort for those people and for others who notice their discomfort. It can also get you into trouble. Avoid using any of the words that are no-no's on network TV. Do not make jokes that point fun at individuals or specific groups, such as women, older people, people with disabilities, or people from ethnic, religious, or racial groups. Demonstrate respect by keeping your language at a professional level at all times.

Some use overly formal language—long, unfamiliar words—when simple, easy-to-understand words would convey the message more quickly. Conversely, some use slang—language that is either unfamiliar or far too casual for the audience. Avoid the temptation to pepper your presentation with words that you think make you sound educated or knowledgeable, or slang that lets your audience know that you are "cool." Instead, use simple, everyday language that gets the message across without the audience having to stop and think about what you mean. That is particularly important if any of the people in your audience are not native English speakers.

> ## Be Clear, Not Simplistic
>
> In *The Group Trainer's Handbook*, David Leigh cautions trainers not to talk down to their adult learners—not to confuse simplicity with simplistic. I find that trainers sometimes do that when they are trying to explain something that they do not fully understand themselves or something that they had difficulty learning. When you are delivering training, never lose sight of the fact that you are talking to adults, not young children. Just because a concept or process is new to people doesn't mean that they need it explained in baby talk. Break things down, spell them out, present information in manageable chunks, and use clear language, but always with a great respect for the audience's ability to learn.

Pronunciation. The people who deliver the television news might differ in the way in which they pronounce some words, but you will almost always be able to understand them easily. It's their job to communicate clearly, and that means using standard speech and speaking distinctly. In ordinary conversation, we often slur words together, using "hafta" instead of "have to," "shoulda" instead of "should have," "meecha later" instead of "meet you later." We also have a tendency to end our sentences with unnecessary tags, such as "y'know?" and "that kinda stuff." That kind of pronunciation might be fine when you are chatting with a colleague in the hall, but it comes across as sloppy in a workshop. Worse, when you slur your words together and fail to pronounce words distinctly, some participants—particularly those who speak English as a second language and those who are hard of hearing—are likely to miss some of what you have to say.

To Improve Your Speaking Skills

Here are some suggestions for making sure that you speak so that you can be easily heard and understood.

- *Learn what you sound like.* Few of us have a realistic understanding of how we sound to others. We hear our own voices differently, for one thing. So the first step in improving your speaking skills is to find out what you sound like when you speak. Make an audio or video recording of yourself speaking as if you were giving a presentation. Ask a colleague or two to watch you deliver part of a presentation and give you feedback. Identify what you need to change, and then practice, practice, practice, until you feel comfortable and at ease with your speaking style.

- *Watch for signs that people can't hear or follow you.* Sometimes trainers begin a presentation with the right volume and pacing, then drop their voice levels and speed up their speech as the workshop goes on. If people start squinting toward you with quizzical looks on their faces or whispering to their neighbors, you might need to adjust your volume or pace. It's always all right to say, "Please let me know if you have trouble hearing me" or to ask, "Can everyone hear me okay?"

- *Think about your audience.* Does it include any people for whom English is a second language? If so, take special care with your word choice, pace, and pronunciation, and use visuals to reinforce key points. Consider whether people are likely to understand the technical terminology associated with the subject, and be sure to define any unfamiliar terminology that you need to use.

Microphone or Not?

Some trainers routinely use microphones and some use them only when addressing a very large group. There are advantages and disadvantages: Using a microphone means that you won't have to worry about whether people can hear you, even when your back is momentarily to the audience, but microphones can separate you from the learners, and they have a tendency to develop annoying screeches.

Here are some things to think about when considering the use of a microphone:

- Unless your voice is unusually soft, avoid using a microphone with a small group in a small room. Aside from technical issues, the microphone might get in the way of establishing rapport with the participants.
- Use the smallest, most unobtrusive microphone you can find, one that makes your voice sound as natural as possible, clips onto your clothing, and has no cords for you to trip over.
- Practice using the microphone in the training room, and ask someone to help you find the right levels.
- The day of the workshop, test the microphone before participants arrive to make sure that it is working properly.
- As mentioned in Chapter 5, practice delivering the workshop without the microphone in case it malfunctions and you have to rely on your voice alone.

Delivering Training Workshops: Pfeiffer Essential Guides to Training Basics.
Copyright © 2010 by John Wiley & Sons, Inc.
Reproduced by permission of Pfeiffer, an Imprint of Wiley. www.Pfeiffer.com

4. Using Equipment, Visual Aids, and Media

Of all the training workshops and seminars that I've attended, one stands out—and not because it was the most interesting or gave me the most valuable information. I can't even remember what the subject was. What I do remember was the trainer's behavior, which was so amazingly distracting that it was like watching an old slapstick comedy routine. Not only did he fiddle with his hair and clothing as he spoke, but he dropped things on the floor. He tripped over electric cords, eliciting gasps from the participants, who thought he had injured himself. He knocked over the flip-chart easels. He couldn't get the DVD into the DVD player. He paced back and forth in front of the slide projector while he spoke, throwing his shadow on the screen. When he wrote on flip-chart pages, he twisted his body into such an uncomfortable-looking position that I kept expecting him to throw his back out. At one point we watched with horror as he inadvertently drew on his shirt with an uncapped marking pen.

That trainer's behavior was extreme. Participants will generally forgive you for dropping a marking pen on the floor, tripping on a cord, fumbling with a piece of equipment, or turning your back from time to time. But awkward, annoying behavior that continues will distract the participants' attention from learning. Worse, it is likely to make you appear weak, disorganized, and less credible.

The more facile you are with the equipment, visual aids, and media, the more professional you will appear and the more confidence you will project. Here are a few suggestions. You'll find lots more in some of the books on the resource list at the back of the book.

Prepare in Advance

When you are preparing yourself to deliver the workshop, set up your laptop so you can practice with the slides. If you'll be using DVDs and CDs, practice starting and stopping them. Set up a flip-chart easel and practice writing on flip-chart pages during key segments. Also make sure that you know how to use any other equipment that will be part of the workshop.

On the day of the workshop, set up your laptop and the projector so that the first slide is ready to show. Make sure the remote controls and any laser pointer you are using are working. Check the brightness and set the controls on your laptop so that it won't go to sleep. Cue up any DVDs or CDs you plan to use and check the sound level. Make sure the flip-chart easels are stable and unlikely to wobble or collapse while you're writing; have enough paper; and are placed where everyone can see them. Check the marking pens to make sure they have enough ink.

Using Slides

When you show slides, face the audience, not the slides, and stand where you are unlikely to block the screen. If you need to see what's on a slide, take a quick glance, and then turn your attention back to the audience. If you will need to refer to slides often during the workshop, print out copies and keep them with your script or instructor notes.

Leave slides up long enough for people to read them. Turn off the screen when you have finished referring to a slide and will not be showing another for a while. When leaving a slide up for participants to refer to during an activity, try not to walk between the slide projector and the screen while you move around the room. Turn the laser pointer off when you're not using it so you don't inadvertently wave it around.

Using Flip Charts

It takes practice and attention to use flip charts so that everyone can see what's being recorded and so that their use does not become distracting. Here are some pointers:

- Write in large block letters that can be read from the back of the room. Use red, yellow, and orange making pens only for highlighting—those colors are hard to see. Use different colors on different lines to make it easier for people to distinguish between items.

- Cap the pens when they are not in use so they do not dry out, and put them down so that you do not wave them around and inadvertently write on yourself. Use pens with washable ink because they do not bleed through the paper and you can wash it if it does get on your hands and clothes.

- Tear off and post any pages that you plan to refer so you don't have to search for them when you need them.

- Try to keep the words you write on a flip-chart page on straight lines. That's easier if you use flip-chart sheets that have faint blue lines.

- When writing on flip-chart pages, do not keep your back to the audience any longer than necessary. Instead, write, turn back to the group, and then talk. Be careful not to block the easel while people are trying to see what's written on the page.

- When recording what participants say, summarize to capture the gist, using the participant's words, when possible, not yours. Use common abbreviations to save writing time and space on the page: "Abt" or "Re" instead of "about"; "co" instead of "company"; "info" instead of "information"; "$$" instead of "money." But use an abbreviation only if you're pretty sure that people will understand what the abbreviation stands for. You can also use symbols such as "&" and leave out articles such as "the" and "a" if you're sure that the meaning is clear without them.

- As needed, check your understanding of what a participant said: "Does this capture what you said?" "Do you mean . . . ?" "What you are saying is . . . ?"

- Thank people for their contributions: "That's a great idea." "Thanks for that."

- Follow brainstorming rules: don't judge contributions—write everything down and then evaluate the list.

- Don't try to squeeze too much information onto a flip-chart page. When a page is full, tear it off and post it and start a new one.

- If you have a lot of things to record or it's very important to maintain your focus on the participants, consider using an assistant for flip-chart work or asking for participants to volunteer.

- When the workshop is over, throw away any flip-chart pages on which you have written confidential or sensitive information.

Look for Opportunities to Practice

Becoming better at delivering workshops takes attention and practice. Look for opportunities to make presentations, even if they are not focused on training. Every time you get up in front of a group, think about what you'd like to focus on. Evaluate your progress regularly by assessing your strengths and weaknesses, obtaining feedback, and, when possible, viewing videos of yourself in action.

Whiteboards

Unless a whiteboard has an electronic feature to capture and print out what's written on it, use whiteboards only for information that doesn't have to be preserved. Don't erase the board until everyone has had a chance to note pertinent information—and use only Dry Erase markers or you will find it difficult to erase what you've written. If you put any confidential or sensitive information on a whiteboard, be sure to erase it completely when the workshop is over.

DVDs

Put DVDs in the DVD player before the workshop begins so they are ready to go and check the sound levels. Make sure that everyone can see the monitor—if necessary, arrange to have two monitors in the room. When you start the DVD, check the sound level again.

Delivery Tips for Virtual Workshops

Like any other workshop, delivering virtual workshops requires keeping track of lots of things at once—they're just different kinds of things or done a little differently. Here are some things to keep in mind when delivering training in a virtual classroom:

- *Use the visuals to keep people's attention and focus them on the content.* Unlike a "regular" workshop, where the visuals support the presentation and discussions, in a virtual workshop the focus is on the screen. The participants' attention is likely to wander if you leave the same slide up too long while you are talking, the visuals are boring, or what's on the screen is not relevant to the content. In general, put such information as key learning points, questions for participants, instructions for activities, and examples on slides; use the whiteboard to capture points during discussions and use highlighting and underlining tools to call attention to important points and keep the screen lively.

- *Avoid rambling discussions or presentations.* People are likely to start checking their e-mail or slip out for a cup of coffee when the presenter in a virtual workshop speaks too long or a discussion goes off track. Keep your own presentation brief and to the point, and step in quickly if a participant begins to ramble: "Excuse me, Jonas, that's a great point, but we don't have much time today, so we need to move on." "Thanks for that, Miranda. In the interest of time, I'm going to move on to the next topic."

- *Speak clearly and distinctly, and watch your tone.* A big disadvantage of a virtual workshop is that you can't see body language or facial expressions that can indicate confusion or lack of attention. For that reason, it's extremely important to avoid speaking too quickly or too slowly, muttering, running your words together, or speaking in a monotone.

- *If you are "on camera"—meaning that participants can see you—stay seated in one position and look right into the camera when you speak.* I recently participated in a virtual workshop in which the trainer kept leaping to his feet and moving around. That movement was incredibly annoying. Trainers who use body language and movement to enhance their presentations in live, in-person workshops don't always realize that it's very distracting to watch a trainer bounce around on the screen and move in and out of the frame.

Quick Quiz

List the three to five key learning points from this chapter that will be most helpful to you.

_____

_____

_____

_____

_____

What's Next?

In a learner-centered classroom, the trainer's primary job is not to deliver information but to help people learn. In the next chapter, you'll learn some strategies for doing just that.

Apply What You Learn

Complete the self-assessment on page 166 to evaluate your delivery skills. Then answer these questions:

1. In what skills are you the strongest?

_____

_____

_____

2. What skills would you like to improve?

_____

_____

_____

3. Which two or three skills will you address first? What will you do to improve them?

_____

_____

_____

_____

_____

_____

_____

Answers to Exercises

Check What You Know

Which trainer appears confident and enthusiastic about the workshop? Which do not? How can you tell? *Your responses may differ.*

Trainer 1

❏ Confident and enthusiastic

Trainer 1 seems to be tired and unhappy, slumping, looking down.

_____

_____

_____

_____

Trainer 2

❏ Confident and enthusiastic

Trainer 2's closed posture indicates that she might not feel very

sure of herself or lacks confidence.

Not balanced on feet .

_____

_____

_____

___ X___ Trainer 3

The third trainer's body language and facial expression

convey an impression of being confident and

enthusiastic.

_____

_____

_____

Check What You Know

Which of the following statements would you agree with?

1. _X_ For people who have a natural tendency to speak softly, raising their voices above the level of normal speech may feel like shouting.
2. ___ The most common tendency among trainers is to speak too slowly.
3. _X_ People who are not used to speaking in public often speak in a monotone.
4. ___ Using formal language, complicated words, jargon, and technical terminology helps trainers appear more educated and credible.
5. _X_ The casual pronunciation we use in everyday speech, such as "hafta" instead of "have to," can seem sloppy in a workshop.

Training Delivery Skills Self-Assessment

This questionnaire will help you to identify your strengths and the areas in which you would like to improve. Complete the assessment yourself. Then, for a more objective assessment, ask a colleague or two to use the assessment to give you feedback on your delivery a workshop. Compare the responses to identify what changes you could make in your delivery.

RATING SCALE

1 = rarely, if ever	3 = often
2 = sometimes	4 = nearly always

1. _____ The clothing I wear is appropriate for the group and presents a professional appearance.

2. _____ I establish rapport by smiling and making eye contact with participants.

3. _____ I appear credible because I am well organized and well prepared, and I have a good understanding of the material.

4. _____ I listen actively when participants are speaking.

5. _____ My gestures are natural and relaxed.

6. _____ I am able to cope with feelings of anxiety and nervousness so that they do not interfere with the workshop.

7. _____ I present information clearly, using language that participants can easily understand.

8. _____ My voice is strong and carries to the back of the room.

9. _____ I pronounce my words clearly.

10. _____ The pace of my speech is not too fast, not too slow, but just about right.

11. _____ I use silence to let participants gather their thoughts before responding to a question.

12. _____ I convey self-confidence and enthusiasm to the group.

13. _____ I avoid talking to the flip chart when writing.

14. _____ I avoid distracting behaviors such as fiddling with my clothes, touching my face, making too many gestures, shifting from foot to foot, or pacing.

15. _____ I am sensitive to cultural differences in body language and gesture.

16. _____ I avoid disconnects between my body language, facial expression, and gestures and my words.

17. _____ I use language that workshop participants can easily understand.

18. _____ I avoid offensive and inappropriate language.

19. _____ I use a conversational tone.

20. _____ I use equipment, visual aids, and media in a way that supports training and does not distract or annoy participants.

Delivering Training Workshops: Pfeiffer Essential Guides to Training Basics.
Copyright © 2010 by John Wiley & Sons, Inc.
Reproduced by permission of Pfeiffer, an Imprint of Wiley. www.Pfeiffer.com

8

Helping People Learn

Check What You Know

"I'm concerned about what I can do so that people actually learn something in the meeting planning workshop," Cybelle told Leon. "I know the point of the whole thing is for them to be able to achieve the learning objectives and then put what they learn to use."

"You're right," Leon told her. "Why hold a workshop unless people come out knowing more than they knew going in?"

"But I'm not sure what to do to help them learn," Cybelle said.

"Your job," Leon said, "is to establish and maintain an environment in which people are able to learn. Let me give you some strategies for doing that."

What do you think Leon might have told Cybelle? What are some of those strategies he might have given her?

_____

_____

_____

_____

_____

_____

Before new teachers receive their credentials, they take classes in teaching methodology and spend time working in a classroom, learning from experienced teachers. That's not always true for people who teach adults. I remember talking with a highly regarded professor, a woman who regularly drew hundreds of students to her college lectures, who had just started teaching a course for executives at a university extension program. "They just stare at me when I ask a question," she complained. "And whenever I do manage to get a discussion going, the same three people do all the talking and I can't get a word in. I don't think I'm cut out for this." That professor knew a lot about teaching. What she didn't know was what she needed to do to help people learn.

Here's what we'll discuss in this chapter:

- How to create a positive learning environment
- How to use questions to engage people, stimulate discussions, and increase learning
- How to monitor and support learning activities

1. Create a Positive Learning Environment

The learning outcomes of teaching cannot be assumed or taken for granted.

Maryellen Weimer, *Learner-Centered Teaching*

Check What You Know

Which statements accurately describe the characteristics of adult learners?

1. _____ Adults prefer being told what to learn so that they won't waste time on learning unimportant things.
2. _____ Adults learn well by trying new ways of doing things in a safe environment.

> 3. _____ Adults learn best when they are able to participate actively in the learning process and discover things on their own.
> 4. _____ Most adults have essentially the same learning preferences and process information in essentially the same way.
> 5. _____ Adults need to see the relevance of what they are learning to their "real" world.

An understanding of how adults learn is an important prerequisite to being able to establish and maintain a positive environment in which they *can* learn. As you develop yourself as a trainer, you will find it useful to learn about the adult learning theories that form the foundation of most successful training programs. In this chapter, we will examine some of the basics. To learn more, consult some of the resources listed at the end of this book.

> *If people don't understand why they are learning something, only 10 to 23 percent of individuals will do something different as a result of training. . . . The clearer the participants' expectations are for what they want to get out of the training, the greater the chance that they will achieve those expectations.*

Ken Blanchard, "Ignite" newsletter, October 2005

There are several key principles to consider when seeking the best ways to help people learn:

Adults need to be actively engaged and involved, and they need to see the relevance of what they are learning. That's the reason for the recurrent theme in this book: successful workshops are not focused on the trainers, they are focused on the learners. Your primary job as a trainer is not to deliver information but to guide the learning process. You do that by encouraging people to participate actively; to discover things on their own, relate what they are learning to what they already know, their previous experiences, and their real world; and to work collaboratively so they can learn from one another.

- People learn by trying things out, making mistakes, and trying again. That's not just true of adults, of course—watch a two-year-old playing with her toys, and you'll see what I mean. We don't learn by listening to people talk or watching people do things; listening and watching provide useful information about how something is done, but in the end, we learn by doing it ourselves. A tennis player tries out all the movements in a serve and then serves the ball over and over again until he can get it into the box with the requisite speed; a mechanic watches someone take an engine out of a car and put it back in again until she has some understanding of how it's done, then tries herself, over and over again until she gets it right; a manager listens to a discussion of the components of feedback, watches a video of people giving feedback, then tries it himself, over and over, until he feels comfortable with the process.

- For adults to take the risks involved in learning something new, they need an environment in which they feel safe, one in which they can experiment without being judged or found lacking. They need feedback and positive reinforcement to help them through the confusion, lack of understanding, and awkwardness that are part of the learning process. They need to know what they are doing right, and what they need to do differently. Knowing that they have mastered even a small part of a process can keep them going.

Each of us has an individual preferred way of learning that suits us best. When you learn the techniques that exactly match your personal learning style, you will be learning in the way that is most natural for you. Because it is natural, it is easier; because it is easier, it is faster.

Accelerated Learning.net, FAQs

- People prefer to learn in different ways. Some people like to learn by watching and listening; others prefer to talk, touch, or move when they are learning. Some process information quickly, others more slowly. Some are comfortable working in groups, others prefer to learn on their own. One of the most important things I discovered as a trainer—and it took me a while—was that not everyone learned in the same way that I did, processed information in the same way, and had the same learning preferences. Successful trainers recognize and respect people's differences in learning preferences and styles, and they provide enough variety in instructional approaches to meet their participants' differing needs.

Your Learning Preferences

How do you learn best? What are your own learning preferences? Understanding the ways in which you prefer to learn helps you recognize when someone learns in a different way than you do. Which statements best describe you?

- ❏ I prefer to listen to a lecture rather than work with a group to draw key learning points from a case study.
- ❏ I speak up quickly in workshops and meetings.
- ❏ I prefer to listen to other people's ideas before speaking up myself.
- ❏ I understand more easily when a verbal presentation is accompanied by visuals.
- ❏ Making lots of notes help me remember what a trainer or speaker says.
- ❏ I prefer quiet, individual activities to interacting with a group.
- ❏ I prefer interacting with a group to working on my own.
- ❏ I like to understand exactly how to do something before trying it out myself.
- ❏ I prefer to jump right in and try things, even if I make mistakes or do it wrong at first.
- ❏ I like to participate in role-play activities.
- ❏ I dislike role-play activities.
- ❏ I don't mind sitting still for long periods if a presentation or discussion is interesting.
- ❏ Even when a presentation or discussion is interesting, I prefer to get up and move around as often as possible.
- ❏ I prefer physical activities to those that involve analyzing and thinking.
- ❏ I prefer activities that involve analyzing and thinking to physical activities.

2. Using Questions

To accomplish their work, artists need tools such as brushes and other implements for spreading paint on a surface. A trainer's most valuable tools are questions. Questions are crucial for engaging people in the learning process, stimulating the discussions that form the heart of nearly every workshop, helping them discover key learning points for themselves, and helping them relate their own experiences and knowledge to the content. In addition, the participants' responses to questions lets you focus the workshop more closely on their needs—for example, they can help you see where you can skip content that people already know or alert you to the need to clarify something.

Among other things, questions help you do the following:

Keep participants engaged. Even people who prefer to learn by listening may have difficulty staying engaged during long lectures. When you need to present content in the form of a lecture, make it interactive by peppering it with such questions as, "Has anyone had that experience? Could you tell us about it?" "Why is that important?" "What if . . . ?" "Who can think of a reason for . . . ?"

- *Stimulate and guide discussions.* You can use questions to get a discussion started and keep it going in the right direction. You might ask a general question such as, "What are ways in which learning to delegate benefits managers?" and then shape the discussion by asking, "If delegating benefits managers in so many ways, what are some reasons that some managers find it difficult to delegate?"

- *Help people relate what they already know to the subject.* You can use questions to help people learn by connecting their prior knowledge and experience with the subject: "What was your best experience with delegating? What made it such a good experience? What does that tell you about how to delegate effectively?"

- *Help people examine the different sides of an issue.* A question can trigger a discussion or debate that helps people think something through and come up with their own conclusions: "When they are delegating, should managers tell people how to do the job, or just give them the goal and let them figure out how to do it on their own? Why or why not?"

- *Help participants discover key learning points on their own.* Instead of telling people what they should do to accomplish a goal, you can ask a question that helps them discover the process for themselves: "Suppose you were delegating the job of setting up a three-day off-site conference to someone who had never done that job before. What would you need to do and say to help the person achieve the right results?"

> ## Use Questions to Make Lectures Interactive
>
> According to Sivasailam "Thiagi" Thiagarajan, author of *Thiagi's Interactive Lectures*, lectures are often "dull and boring … passively received information is often soon forgotten [and] real learning requires active participation." Thiagi recommends interspersing lecture content with activities that help participants to review, summarize, and reflect on what they hear, and think about how they can apply it.

THINK ABOUT IT

Notice the differences between the ways in which these questions are phrased. Which questions would be most likely to trigger productive discussions?

1. _____ Do you think that grammar and punctuation errors matter in a press release?
2. _____ What do you think the results of grammar and punctuation errors in a press release might be?
3. _____ How many of you agree that a press release should be free of grammar and punctuation errors?
4. _____ What are some reasons for making sure that a press release should be free of grammar and punctuation errors?

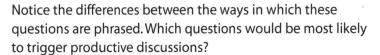

What's a Useful Question?

You probably noticed that Question 1 above can be answered with a "yes" or a "no," and that Question 3 could be answered with a show of hands. Those are "closed-ended" questions. Although closed-ended questions can sometimes be useful, they do little to stimulate either thinking or discussion.

Question 2 is an "open-ended" question, one that cannot be answered with a simple "yes" or "no." This form of a question asks people to think widely and to consider all the possible results. Question 4, which is also open-ended, asks people to think and would be useful for triggering a discussion, but it includes an assumption—that press releases *should* be free of errors—that would narrow the conversation.

Here are some guidelines for making the best use of questions:

- *Establish the expectation that you will be asking questions right from the beginning of the workshop.* During the opening, you might say: "I'll be asking you lots and lots of questions today. The questions are designed to help you understand and think about the material. Please respond even if you aren't sure about the answer. There is usually no one right answer. Even when there is, you can learn even more from the wrong answers than the right ones." Immediately follow the explanation with a question or two so that people can become comfortable with the process.

Ask mostly open-ended questions, those that cannot be answered by "yes" or "no." Use closed-ended questions such as, "Have you read the new safety regulations?" or "Who has read the new safety regulations?" only when you want "yes" or "no" responses or a show of hands. To elicit ideas, opinions, or information, ask open-ended questions, such as, "Which of the safety regulations have you read?" or "Can anyone describe the new safety regulations?"

THINK ABOUT IT

Put a check mark in front of the closed-ended questions. Then reword them so they are open-ended.

1. ☐ Do you think that you always need to send out an agenda before a meeting?

   _____

2. ☐ What are the seven steps in the problem-solving process?

   _____

3. ☐ Is the online customer service manual the best place to find an answer to a customer's question about our refund policy?

   _____

4. ☐ Who is familiar with the procedures for submitting expense reports?

   _____

5. ☐ When is it most useful to make decisions by consensus?

   _____

Plan the initial questions in advance. Look through the script or trainer notes for places where you could ask a question to obtain information from participants, start them thinking about something, or stimulate a discussion. Write out those questions. You will probably ask more questions to probe further or keep a discussion going, but writing out the initial questions gives you a starting place. If you are using a script that includes questions, look closely at them to see whether any rewording might make them more useful, and add any other questions that might help to engage and involve the participants.

Think about what responses you expect. Knowing why you're asking a question and what response or responses you're looking for helps you focus the question, recognize when it has been answered, and fill in any key points that participants do not mention. If you plan to ask, "What do you think the results of not making expectations clear when you delegate might be?" Make a note of some results that you expect participants to mention, such as the person being unable to do the job to your satisfaction. If you plan to ask, "What are some advantages to making decisions by consensus?" Make a note of some advantages that you expect participants to come up with, such as an increased level of commitment to carrying out the decision.

Avoid leading questions. If you watch courtroom dramas like *Law and Order*, you know that trial attorneys "lead" people on the stand to the responses they want: "Isn't it true, Mr. Smith, that you stood to benefit from your wife's death because you would inherit her estate?" Trainers also tend to ask leading questions: "Isn't the first step in solving a problem to figure out what the problem really is so that you don't waste time and effort solving the wrong problem?" But leading questions are not very useful in training—for people to learn, they need to come up with their own answers. A better question would be: "What is the first step in the problem-solving process, and why is that step important?"

Be patient and don't answer your own questions. Sometimes people eagerly jump in with responses even before you've finished asking a question. But when they don't, you might feel a need to answer it yourself. Resist that urge. Wait ten seconds or so to give people time to consider their responses. If no one responds, you might need to repeat and clarify the question. Answer it yourself only if it becomes clear that the participants are unable to do so.

Ask only one question at a time. Trainers have a tendency to pile question on question: "Who has had this kind of experience? What was the result? What do you think you could have done to prevent the problem in the first place?" Those are all good questions, but they would be difficult to answer all at once. Give people a chance to answer the first one before asking the second, and so on.

Build on the responses. To encourage participants to provide more information or examine an issue in more depth, ask follow-up questions:

"That's an interesting point. What else can you tell us about . . . ?" "What do you think might have happened if . . . ?

- *Show respect for the participants, no matter what.* Never, ever scoff at an answer or put someone down. It takes courage to venture a response to a question. Honor people for that courage. Never ask trick questions, those designed to elicit incorrect answers, and never make fun of a response (unless the participant has laughed first).

- *Help people out if they have trouble articulating a response.* Some people know what they want to say but have difficulty getting the words out. Give them enough time to try, but if they really seem to be having trouble, gently help out by clarifying: "Brendon, are you saying that . . . ?" "Let me see if I understand, Maria. You are saying that. . . ."

- *Let people choose whether to respond.* Pose questions to the entire group, instead of to one person, especially at the start of a workshop before people have had time to develop confidence and trust. If no one responds, look for nonverbal cues that let you know someone has an answer at the ready but may be unsure about speaking up: perhaps someone is leaning slightly forward and making eye contact with you. Then you might say, "Janet, would you like to tell us what you think about . . . ?" As a general rule, avoid asking questions that begin with "why," because they can put people on the defensive. Instead of asking, "Why does the team have trouble making decisions?" ask, "What are some reasons the group seems to have trouble . . ."?

- *Rephrase questions to which you receive no response.* For people to answer a question, they need to be able to understand it. If no one responds to a question and you see puzzled looks on people's faces, rephrase the question and ask it again. If you still receive no response, the question might have made people uncomfortable, or they might be unwilling to speak up in the group. If you think it's appropriate and the question is an important one, try asking it another way: "Let me rephrase that . . ." or "It seems as if we need to take a closer look at what might be going on." Otherwise, you can give the answer yourself and move on, or just move on.

- *Make sure that everyone hears and understands the responses.* It's not only frustrating for workshop participants when they cannot hear someone's response to a question, but they might miss important information or ideas. But some people speak too softly to be heard, especially by those at the back of the room. Unless you are certain that everyone has heard, repeat the response: "Alan said that one reason for. . . ." Also, clarify or summarize vague or lengthy responses: "Let me see if I've got that right, Margot. You suggest that. . . ." Also repeat—and if necessary, clarify—responses when people's accents make it hard to understand what they say.

Give Everyone a Chance to Answer Questions

There are participants whose hands shoot up the moment a question is asked and those who like to mull things over before responding. To give everyone a chance to participate, you need to help the second group out a little. Here are some ways in which you can do that:

- After asking a question, say, "Think about that for a moment." Wait for a few seconds, then ask, "Who would like to address that question?" and call on someone who hasn't spoken recently.
- Use a round-robin format for responses. Say, "Let's hear from Table 1 on this" or "Can someone at Table 2 give us an example of . . . ?"
- Elicit more than one response to the same question. After the first person speaks, say, "Alicia, that's a great idea. Who has another suggestion?"
- Ask people who respond to a question to wait until at least one other person has responded before they speak up again.

Asking Useful Questions

- Plan questions in advance.
- Think about what responses you expect.
- Avoid leading questions.
- Be patient and don't answer your own questions.
- Ask only one question at a time.
- Build on the responses.
- Show respect for the participants, no matter what.
- Help people out if they have trouble articulating a response.
- Let people choose whether to respond.
- Rephrase questions to which you receive no response.
- Make sure that everyone hears and understands the responses.

Incorporate Examples and Stories in Discussions

There are lots of very good reasons to use examples and stories in training. According to Terrence L. Gargiulo, author of *Once Upon a Time: Using Story-Based Activities to Develop Breakthrough Communication Skills*, "Stories are how we communicate, learn, and think." Giving a brief personal example or a story from your own experience before asking a question of the participants is a good way to help them open up. Encouraging people to share their own examples and stories helps them connect the topic of the discussion with their own experiences and those of their colleagues.

3. Monitor and Support Individual and Small-Group Work

Check What You Know

Which statements describe effective strategies for monitoring and supporting individual and small-group activities during a workshop?

1. _____ To keep people from becoming frustrated, monitor activities as closely as possible so you can step in right away if they run into trouble.
2. _____ Avoid telling people what they are doing wrong and what they are doing right.
3. _____ When monitoring activities, keep in mind that your primary role is that of an observer and a guide.
4. _____ When you introduce the activity, be careful to explain what people are supposed to learn.
5. _____ If possible, stay out of the room during activities so that people won't feel self-conscious with you looking on.

The "work" in workshop is important. Much of the learning that occurs during a workshop occurs during individual and small-group activities in which participants learn through discovery and practice new skills and techniques. Your role as trainer is to facilitate that learning by making sure that people understand how to do the activity and remaining available to monitor and support them as they work. Here's how:

- *Introduce the activity and give clear instructions.* Before beginning an activity, participants need to know why they are doing it, what they are supposed to do, and how long it will take: "For the next thirty minutes, you will work in small groups to explore strategies for. . . ." "In the time we have left before we break for lunch, I'd like you to work with a partner to plan a meeting." If the instructions are complicated, put them in the participant workbook, on a handout, and/or on a flip-chart page or slide. Give participants a chance to ask questions before the activity begins.

- *Avoid telling people what they are supposed to learn from an activity.* The purpose of many small-group and individual activities is for the participants to discover something on their own. It defeats the purpose if you tell them ahead of time what they are supposed to learn.

- *Remain available while people do the activity.* Just because participants are working on their own doesn't mean that you should disappear. Once you've set up the activity and clarified the instructions, stay out of their way for a few minutes while they get started. But if you leave the room, come back quickly enough so that you can make sure that they're on track and be available to help if they have trouble. Circulate around the room to answer questions, listen in on discussions, and observe what's happening.

- *Be unobtrusive.* When monitoring activities, your role is that of observer and guide, not participant. When you move up to a small group, people are likely to stop talking and focus their attention on you. They might even start explaining what they are doing. Say, "Keep on going. I'd just like to listen for a moment." If you can, pull a chair a little back from the group and sit down so they forget that you're there.

- *Wait before offering help.* Be careful not to jump in too quickly if you see that people are confused or doing something incorrectly—muddling through is part of the learning process. But if it's clear that they are seriously off track, offer help. Avoid telling them what they are doing wrong and how to do it right. Instead, ask questions like, "You seem to be stuck. What do you think is going on?" "What are some ways in which you could . . . ?"

- *Help participants keep track of time.* When you give participants instructions for the activity, tell them how much time they will have and what time it will be when the activity is over: "You'll have thirty minutes to discuss the case. We'll reconvene at 11:15." Give them a time check when they are halfway through and a warning a few minutes before the time is up.

- *Help people think about what they have learned.* The purpose of an activity is not the activity itself but what people learn from engaging in it. After an activity, help participants examine what happened, reflect on what they learned, relate what they learned to real-world situations, and think about how they can apply the learning. For example, you might ask them to answer questions in their workbooks or give them questions to discuss: "During this activity, what did you notice about the way in which your group went about making the decision?" "What part of the process worked well, and what part did not? Why do you think that was?" "What common themes or general principles did you notice?" "What did you learn about yourself from this process?" "What did you learn from this experience that you can use to help your team make better decisions?" "What will you/your team do differently as a result of this experience?"

Delivering Training Workshops: Pfeiffer Essential Guides to Training Basics.
Copyright © 2010 by John Wiley & Sons, Inc.
Reproduced by permission of Pfeiffer, an Imprint of Wiley. www.Pfeiffer.com

Experiential Learning

The most useful activities for a workshop follow David Kolb's experiential learning model, which guides learners through the process of answering three important questions: "What?" "So What?" "Now What?"

- "WHAT happened during this activity? What did you feel? What did you notice?" For example, learners in a workshop on team problem solving might say, "We never bothered to talk about why this problem needs to be solved" or "Every time one of us came up with an idea, someone else shot it down."
- "SO WHAT did you learn from this experience? How do you see the problem-solving process differently? What have you learned that will help you improve the way you go about solving problems?" Learners in the problem-solving workshop might say, "To keep from wasting time, we need to start by determining what might happen if we ignore the problem" or "To come up with good solutions, we need to listen to and consider every possibility, even if it sounds unworkable or silly at first."
- "NOW WHAT can you do with this learning? In what ways can you take what you learned into the 'real' world? How will it help you?" The learners in the problem-solving workshop might say, "When we have identified an apparent problem, we'll start by figuring out whether we really need to address it—what might happen if we do nothing" or "When we brainstorm possible solutions, we'll write down every idea before evaluating them."

An experiential activity generally includes these components:

1. *The introduction.* First, tell learners what they are going to do and why they are going to do it, and give them any instructions they will need. Although the introduction might include a *brief* explanation of a theory or concept or some kind of demonstration, be careful not to tell them what they are supposed to learn.
2. *The activity.* While participants engage in the activity, monitor their work to provide guidance they might need to stay on the right track.
3. *The debriefing (processing).* Help people make sense of what they have experienced, done, or observed, and connect the learning to their own experiences. This is an essential part of the experience; without it, the activity may have little or no meaning and provide little or no learning.
4. *Application.* The goal of training is to effect change. The purpose of this component is to help learners connect what they have learned to their real world and change the way they do things.

Monitoring and Supporting Individual and Small-Group Work

- Introduce the activity and give clear instructions.
- Remain available.
- Keep people on track.
- Help participants keep track of time.
- Help people think about what they have learned.

Check What You Know

What are some of the ways in which people can participate actively in a virtual workshop?

_____

_____

_____

_____

Tips for Helping People Learn in Virtual Workshops

Participation and interaction is just as important to learning in a virtual workshop as in a live, in-person workshop. The great challenge for trainers who conduct virtual workshops is finding ways to encourage active participation when people cannot see one another and must communicate only with the use of technology. Consider the following:

Learn about the tools you have available and practice until you can manage them easily. To engage and involve participants in a virtual workshop, you will use a variety of tools, such as a whiteboard on which you and the participants can write or draw; desktop sharing, which allows you and the participants to see documents at the same time; a chat window, in which you and the participants can "converse" in real time; surveys and polls, which you can use to ask questions of the participants; and virtual breakout rooms. For the workshop to run smoothly, you need to understand each tool that you have available and learn how to use it with ease.

Plan for interaction and participation. Interaction and participation are natural elements of a live, in-person workshop. Those elements must be carefully planned for in a virtual workshop if it is to be more than a one-way presentation, with the trainer delivering information to a largely passive audience. Go through the workshop script to find places where you can ask a question or insert an activity instead of simply delivering content.

Consider the time you have available. Just as with live, in-person workshops, trainers often sacrifice participation in virtual workshops because they are trying to achieve too many objectives and get across too much content in the time available. Virtual workshops are normally a maximum of sixty to ninety minutes. If you want to encourage interaction and include activities that help people learn, you might have to limit the learning objectives and content.

Promote active involvement right from the beginning. To establish the expectation that this is a learner-centered workshop and help people feel comfortable in the learning environment, get participants talking as soon as they enter the virtual classroom. Greet them by name and ask them a question so that you can make sure their audio links are working. These initial questions also let people hear one another's voices.

Help people learn to use the tools. Unless you know for sure that all the participants are already familiar with the tools used in virtual meeting rooms, give them a quick hands-on tutorial before launching into the opening of the workshop. For example, show them how to raise their hands, use the status icons, answer polling questions, and use the chat function.

Quick Quiz

List the three to five key learning points from this chapter that will be most helpful to you.

_____

_____

_____

_____

_____

Apply What You Learn

Use the worksheet at the end of the chapter to identify ways in which you can create an environment for helping people learn in your workshop.

Answers to Exercises

Check What You Know

Which statements accurately describe the characteristics of adult learners?

1. ___ Adults prefer being told what to learn so that they won't waste time on learning unimportant things.
2. _X_ Adults learn well by trying new ways of doing things in a safe environment.
3. _X_ Adults learn best when they are able to participate actively in the learning process and discover things on their own.
4. ___ Most adults have essentially the same learning preferences and process information in essentially the same way.
5. _X_ Adults need to see the relevance of what they are learning to their "real" world.

THINK ABOUT IT

Notice the differences between the ways in which these questions are phrased. Which questions would be most likely to trigger productive discussions?

1. ___ Do you think that grammar and punctuation errors matter in a press release?
2. _X_ What do you think the results of grammar and punctuation errors in a press release might be?
3. ___ How many of you agree that a press release should be free of grammar and punctuation errors?
4. _X_ What are some reasons for making sure that a press release should be free of grammar and punctuation errors?

THINK ABOUT IT

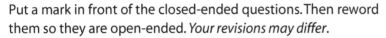

Put a mark in front of the closed-ended questions. Then reword them so they are open-ended. *Your revisions may differ.*

1. _X_ Do you think that you always need to send out an agenda before a meeting?
   In what situations do you need to send out an agenda before a meeting?
2. ___ What are the seven steps in the problem-solving process?
3. _X_ Is the online customer service manual the best place to find an answer to a customer's question about our refund policy?
   Where would you find information to answer a customer's question about our refund policy?
4. _X_ Who is familiar with the procedures for submitting expense reports?
   What are the procedures for submitting expense reports?
5. ___ When is it most useful to make decisions by consensus?

Check What You Know

Which statements would you agree describe effective strategies for monitoring and supporting individual and small-group activities during a workshop?

1. ___ To keep people from becoming frustrated, monitor activities as closely as possible so you can step in right away if they run into trouble.
2. _X_ Avoid telling people what they are doing wrong and what they are doing right.
3. _X_ When monitoring activities, keep in mind that your primary role is that of an observer and a guide.
4. ___ When you introduce the activity, be careful to explain what people are supposed to learn.
5. ___ If possible, stay out of the room during activities so that people won't feel self-conscious with you looking on.

Creating an Environment
That Helps People Learn

1. What will you do to create a positive learning environment for the participants in your workshop? What can you do to engage them in the material and encourage their active participation?

_____

_____

_____

_____

2. What questions could you ask participants to:

   Make lectures more interactive?

   _____

   _____

   Stimulate discussions?

   _____

   _____

   Help people relate what they are learning to their experiences and what they already know?

   _____

   _____

   Help participants discover the key learning points on their own?

   _____

   _____

   Help participants relate what they are learning to their "real" world?

   _____

   _____

9
Managing the Learning Group

Delivering Training Workshops: Pfeiffer Essential Guides to Training Basics.
Copyright © 2010 by John Wiley & Sons, Inc.
Reproduced by permission of Pfeiffer, an Imprint of Wiley. www.Pfeiffer.com

If you think back to your school years, you probably remember some students better than others—the class clown who got everyone in trouble, the bully you tried to stay away from, the show-off whose hand shot into the air the moment the teacher asked a question, the boy who blushed beet red when he was asked to speak, and the girls who continually whispered in a corner of the room. It's a good bet that the teachers would remember those students, too, because they required extra attention so that everyone was able to learn.

One of your most difficult jobs as a trainer is managing the learning group. But your students are adult learners, not children. You can't tell them to stand in a corner, go to the principal's office, or stay after school when they've been disruptive. You can't give them a low grade for not participating. You can't really take away their cell phones (although some trainers do). So what can you do? That's what you'll learn in this chapter. Here are the topics

- Common challenges to managing the group
- How to keep things moving and on track
- How to encourage participation
- How to handle behavior challenges

1. Common Challenges

Sometimes, you can see them walking in the door—the disruptive behaviors. They may be vying for the center of attention, are boisterous, or are negatively outspoken. On the other hand, they may ignore everyone and refuse to make eye contact right from the start. Disruptive behaviors interrupt the flow of the training session and have a negative effect on the positive climate you're trying to create.

Elaine Biech, *Training for Dummies*

THINK ABOUT IT

1. What are some of the challenges that have come up during workshops that you have attended or those that you have delivered?

_____

_____

_____

_____

2. In what ways did those challenges impact everyone's ability to learn?

_____

_____

_____

_____

As you already know, one of your primary responsibilities as a trainer is to maintain an environment that is conducive to learning and keep the workshop on track. That job would be much easier if everything always went as planned and participants were always enthusiastic and cooperative. In my experience, that never happens. There are challenges in even the best situation, and the ways in which you deal with them can affect people's ability to learn and the smooth running of the workshop in significant ways.

Below is an overview of the kinds of challenges that trainers typically face (not in any particular order). In this chapter, you'll learn strategies for dealing with them.

- *Staying on track.* We've all attended workshops during which the trainer has started speeding up as the day progressed, delivering lectures instead of holding discussions, dropping activities off the agenda, and even keeping us beyond the scheduled ending time. So many things can throw even the most carefully planned workshop off track—malfunctioning equipment, getting started late, discussions that run too long. But talking more quickly and leaving out or shortcutting activities does nothing to help the learning process. And people seriously dislike being kept in the training room after the workshop is supposed to be over.

Getting full participation. It can be challenging to get everyone to participate in the discussions and activities that are so important to the learning process. People who resist participating, or who participate only with obvious reluctance, may not only fail to benefit from the training, but they may make others feel uncomfortable. You need to come prepared with a variety of strategies for encouraging participation in ways that respect different learning preferences and comfort levels.

Handling difficult participants. There are certain behaviors that are very annoying, unpleasant, and take up valuable time. These behaviors are distracting at best; at their worst, they can poison the training environment, making it difficult or even impossible for anyone to focus on learning. Participants expect you to manage participants who engage in these behaviors, so you need to be prepared to do so.

Check What You Know

Here are some typical situations you might encounter in a workshop. Which strategy would be the best for handling each situation?

1. _____ One of the workshop participants keeps interrupting other people while they are talking.
   A. Say, "Andrea, you're talking too much. Please stop interrupting everyone."
   B. Ignore the behavior and be grateful for the person's energy and enthusiasm.
   C. Say, "I'd like to remind everyone that we established a ground rule about interrupting while others are talking. Let's try to honor that ground rule."

2. _____ A participant in the back of the room lounges in his chair, never makes eye contact with you, never responds to a question, and refuses to do the activities.
   A. Speak with the person privately during a break.
   B. Make it a point to call on the person by name.
   C. Ignore the behavior as long as he isn't bothering anyone.

3. _____ Two participants keep up a running dialogue with one another while you are speaking.
   A. Stop your presentation and ask, "Albert and Carla, why don't you tell us what's so interesting?"
   B. Continuing to speak, walk in the direction of the talkative participants and stand close to them until they stop talking.
   C. Ignore them for the moment and then call them aside during the next break.

4. _____ Participants are so enthusiastic that discussions are going on too long and veering into interesting directions that are not directly related to the subject of the workshop.
   A. If the discussions are productive, let them go on as long as people are interested, then drop an activity or two to make up for the lost time.
   B. At the beginning of the workshop, set up a parking lot for important issues that come up but are not related to the topic at hand.
   C. Stop every discussion when the time is up, no matter what.

2. How to Keep Things Moving and on Track

"I don't know what happened," a new trainer told me recently. "We were halfway through the workshop and we'd gotten through less than a quarter of the material."

That's not an unusual situation. All it takes is one late start, a malfunctioning projector, an activity that takes longer than expected, a detour onto an interesting side issue, and suddenly you're running behind. It's like what happens when bad weather closes an airport—before long, planes are

Delivering Training Workshops: Pfeiffer Essential Guides to Training Basics.
Copyright © 2010 by John Wiley & Sons, Inc.
Reproduced by permission of Pfeiffer, an Imprint of Wiley. www.Pfeiffer.com

stacked up on runways all over the country. Just as it's nearly impossible for an airline to get back on schedule after a series of delays, it can be very difficult for a trainer to get back on track after losing control of the time.

In earlier chapters, you learned how to avoid certain challenges by sending reminders about the workshop start time; confirming and reconfirming reservations for the facility, the room setup, equipment, and refreshments; and arriving early enough so that everything would be ready when participants arrived. But you can't foresee everything. I've had workshops interrupted by fire drills and power outages, and it's not unusual for people to be called away to deal with emergencies. What's important is to come prepared with backup plans, pay attention to what's going on, deal with problems right away, and be flexible enough to respond to the unexpected.

There are a number of things you need to do to keep things moving and stay on track, including getting started on time, keeping your eye on the time and the agenda, and getting people back on time from breaks. You also need to manage discussions so they do not go on too long and stop activities when the time is up. When planning the agenda, leaving yourself some "wiggle room" and decide what you could drop or do more quickly if you start to run behind.

Check What You Know

In addition to making sure that everything is ready to go when participants arrive, what strategies can you think of for getting a workshop started on time?

_____

_____

_____

_____

Get Started on Time

If you start a workshop late, you'll always be playing catch-up, trying to get that time back. The problem is that your and the participants' idea of what "on time" means might be different. Getting people to arrive on time is an ongoing challenge, especially in organizations in which the culture does not encourage punctuality. But not only does a late start time make it hard to stay on schedule, but starting late isn't fair to those people who do arrive on time. Here are some strategies you might try:

- *Put a cushion in the start time.* Instead of announcing the start time as "9:00," encourage people to arrive early for refreshments. Use this kind of phrasing to announce the start time: "Continental breakfast at 8:45, workshop begins at 9 A.M."

- *Enlist the support of participants' managers.* Earlier in this book, you learned that people usually take training more seriously when they know that their managers consider the workshop important. Checking with managers a few days ahead of time to see whether they have questions about the workshop is one way to remind them that the training is coming up.

- *Send out reminders.* A few days before the workshop, send a note reminding people of the date and time. Include something for them to do—something to bring or a question to think about. The day before or the day of the workshop, send another quick e-mail or text reminder—"See you at the Delegating for Results workshop tomorrow—breakfast at 8:45, workshop begins promptly at 9:00."

- *Use a teaser.* Knowing that something is going to happen right at the beginning of the workshop helps to encourage people to get there on time. Schedule a compelling, engaging activity for the first few minutes of the workshop and tell participants about it in advance.

Keep Your Eye on the Clock and on the Agenda

Delivering a successful workshop requires paying attention to lots of things at once. While you are facilitating discussions, answering questions, and monitoring activities, you not only need to be aware of group dynamics and the behavior of individual participants, but you need to keep track of the time and know exactly where you are in the sequence of content and activities.

Delivering Training Workshops: Pfeiffer Essential Guides to Training Basics.
Copyright © 2010 by John Wiley & Sons, Inc.
Reproduced by permission of Pfeiffer, an Imprint of Wiley. www.Pfeiffer.com

Clocks Versus Watches

I prefer a wall clock to a watch. For one thing, I don't like to make a point of checking to see what time it is. For another, a wall clock with a large face is easier to see. But many of the rooms that people use for training do not have wall clocks, or the ones they have are positioned so that you can't see them without twisting around. Just in case, my box of training supplies includes a small travel clock with a large, easy-to-see display that I can put right on the table with my trainer notes or guide.

To keep track, it helps to have some kind of checklist or "at-a-glance" agenda that includes start and stop times for each segment of the workshop and each activity. The training materials you are using might include that kind of trainer aid. If not, make one of your own. Keep it where you can refer to it easily and check off what you've already done. I also post an agenda on the wall as a kind of road map that lets both me and the participants see where we are on our journey. (I leave the times off that agenda, however, so that people do not get caught up in watching the time or become confused when something takes more or less time than planned.)

Check What You Know

What are some things that a trainer could do to get people to come back on time from breaks?

_____

_____

_____

_____

Get People Back on Time from Breaks

The primary purpose of a break is to let participants use the restrooms and get on their feet for a few minutes. But the moment you announce a break, people tend to disappear into the hallway with their cell phones or run back to their desks. Because their attention is on other things, they often do not notice that the workshop is about to resume.

Trainers go crazy trying to devise strategies for getting people back when breaks are over. In *Creative Training Techniques*, Bob Pike suggests using odd times, such as, "We'll break until 11:06." Some trainers hate breaks so much that they eliminate them altogether, but all that achieves is a roomful of restless, uncomfortable people, many of whom will get up and leave while something else is going on.

Here are some strategies you can try to keep breaks from making you fall behind:

- *Give people just enough time, but not too much.* Some trainers keep breaks very short—five or ten minutes—and then are surprised when people aren't back on time. Breaks should be at least ten minutes long for people to be able to take care of their personal needs and move around a little. For most workshops, I've had the best luck with one fifteen-minute break in the morning and two ten-minute breaks in the afternoon. But keep breaks to a maximum of fifteen minutes. With longer breaks, people tend to disappear or lose focus.

- *Leave some lag time in the agenda.* Assuming that people might not come back on time from a break, leave an extra few minutes in the schedule—for example, when you schedule a ten-minute break, leave an extra three to five minutes. If they come back on time, great—you can always use a few extra minutes. If not, you won't have to sacrifice anything to make up for lost time.

- *Resume the workshop on time after breaks.* Finding that the group is already involved in a discussion or activity when they return to the room encourages some people to get back on time from the next break. You also cannot afford to lose time waiting until all the participants are back in their seats.

- *Set up an "out-the-door" reminder.* Put an easel right next to the door with a flip-chart page that says in large, easy-to-see letters, "Please check your watches and be back by 10:30!"

- *Ask for volunteers to act as "break monitors."* At the beginning of the workshop, explain the importance of getting back from breaks to the smooth running of the workshop and ask a few people to be responsible for rounding up people when the time for a break is just about up.

- *Establish a ground rule.* Include "return on time from breaks" in the ground rules and refer to it as needed.

- *Ask participants to stay in the area.* When people go back to their work stations during breaks, they are likely to forget about the time, or even get caught up in something and not return at all. Ask them to remain in the vicinity of the training room so that they can get back quickly when the break is over.

- *Incorporate breaks into activities.* People are more likely to return from breaks if they are in the middle of something interesting when the break occurs. Wrap group or individual activities around breaks. You can say, "You have thirty-five minutes for this activity. That time includes a ten-minute break, which you can take whenever you'd like." Monitor the activities to make sure that people do take a break before the workshop resumes.

How Long for Lunch?

Trainers sometimes try to save time by giving people less time for lunch. In my experience, workshop participants need a minimum of forty or forty-five minutes if lunch is provided, and at least an hour, perhaps a little more, if they have to leave the facility. It rarely does any good to reduce that time, because not everyone will be there when it's time to start the afternoon session. If you are short on time, consider using part of the lunch time for an activity, such as a group discussion.

Manage Discussions

Discussions form the heart of nearly every workshop. By discussions, I mean any activity in which people share information and ideas with the trainer and with one another. In fact, among the most important benefits of providing training in a live, in-person workshop are the opportunities for the face-to-face discussions that actively engage people in the learning process. Discussions allow people to learn from one another by sharing their knowledge, experiences, ideas, and points of view.

As a good trainer, you want to involve people in discussions. But once discussions are underway, it can be difficult to stop them, as well as to keep them focused on the subject. People sometimes become so interested in a topic that they want to keep talking about it. Discussions often trigger side issues. And sometimes people are just long-winded.

Knowing what you expect a discussion to accomplish helps you recognize when it is going off track. When that happens, you can say something like, "You've come up with some excellent points, but now we seem to be veering in another direction. Let's put those issues in our parking lot and go back to the questions we're trying to address." Once the goal has been achieved, bring the discussion to a close and sum up the key points before moving on: "I think we've had some important insights about. . . . Before we move on, let's review the key points that came out of this conversation."

> ## How to Manage Discussions
> - Know what you want a discussion to accomplish.
> - Recognize when a discussion has gone off track.
> - Put side issues in the parking lot.
> - Close discussion when the goal has baen accomplished.

Manage the Timing of the Activities

When people work on an activity, whether in small groups or on their own, some are likely to finish early, while others won't be finished when the time is up. You can actually count on this happening often, no matter how carefully you estimate the time, and it can be difficult to handle. People who finish early can grow impatient, and others can become frustrated when they do not have enough time to finish.

To stay on schedule, you need to stop activities when the time is up, even if some people are still working. You also need to provide something for the early finishers to do before they disappear into the lobby with their cell phones.

Try the following to manage the timing of the activities:

- When you introduce an activity, tell people how much time they will have and what time the activity will be over. Explain that you understand that some of them might not be finished at that time, but that finishing the activity itself isn't the primary goal.

- While you monitor the activities, notice people who seem to be finished. Check to make sure that they have really done the activity. If they misunderstood an instruction or skipped something, clarify as needed and set them back to work.

- When people finish early, offer another activity, something to read, or a quick break.

- If most of the group is still working when the time is almost up, offer another few minutes if you can. If people still haven't finished when you need to stop, refer to the agenda and say something like, "I can see that you could continue with this, but we've still got a lot to do, so we need to move on. Now, I'd like to know what this experience was like for you. . . ."

- Leave yourself some wiggle room. As mentioned earlier, participants expect workshops to end on time. Just as you need a cushion in the start time and some lag time when you schedule breaks, leave a little extra time before and after activities so you don't have to feel crunched if things go on longer than expected. It's like using an expandable suitcase—you might not need the extra room but it's nice to know it's there.

- In case things go more quickly, no one's likely to complain if you take an extra break or end the workshop a few minutes early.

3. How to Encourage Participation

In order to learn something well, your participants must listen, observe, ask questions, and discuss the material. . . . The success of active training depends on your ability to form and sustain a learning environment in which participants take on the responsibility to be "doers."

Mel Silberman, *Training the Active Way*

After you've been training for a while, certain workshops will stand out in your mind as particularly successful experiences—or the reverse. One of my first workshops was mandatory training in incident report writing for hourly workers at a government agency who didn't much like their boss, their jobs, or one another. A few of them were great—they participated actively and even enthusiastically. But many of them spared no effort in making it clear that they considered the whole thing a complete waste of time. They hid behind newspapers, made jokes, and dozed in their chairs. I tried my best to ignore them.

But not only was their behavior distracting for those people who were interested in learning, but ignoring them took an enormous amount of energy; by the end of the workshop, I felt like a dishrag that had been twisted into knots and wrung out.

Check What You Know

Which of the following statements would you agree with?

1. _____ When a workshop is mandatory, you can expect that most of the people who attend are likely to resist participating actively.
2. _____ People can be participating actively even if they seldom speak up.
3. _____ People's experiences with training can affect their willingness to become engaged and their ability to learn.

As you've already seen, the extent to which people participate actively in a workshop affects more than their own ability to learn—it affects the learning environment as a whole. One of your most important jobs as a trainer—and often your biggest challenge—is encouraging people to participate even when they are reluctant or even unwilling to do so.

But it helps to understand some things about participation before looking for ways of encouraging it. One is that people come to workshops for many reasons, and those reasons do not always include learning. Another is that people participate in different ways, and it's not always immediately obvious whether or not someone is engaged. Still another is that people bring to a workshop their different experiences with training and different ideas about how they are expected to behave in a workshop. Let's look more closely at how those factors affect people's motivation and willingness to participate actively in training, and what you can do to engage them.

Think About Why People Are There

The word "mandatory" strikes fear into a trainer's heart, and for good reason. Like the participants mentioned above who gave me such grief, some people see mandatory training as something to be endured, which can make it especially challenging to engage them. In the same way, it can also be difficult to engage people who have been pressured to attend because of a performance issue. But it's important not to make assumptions. Some people who sign up on their own are only interested in getting away from work for a few hours, not in learning about the topic, while others who have been required or told to attend arrive ready and willing to learn. I've also found that people who are initially suspicious about a workshop and resist becoming involved sometimes end up participating fully and getting a lot out of the experience.

Think About the Different Ways in Which People Participate

When I first started training, I found it very frustrating that, no matter how hard I tried to engage everyone, some people rarely spoke up, never volunteered, and were apparently reluctant to become actively involved in activities. I assumed that those people were not interested in the topic or didn't want to be there for some reason. After all, when I attended a workshop, I enjoyed engaging in discussions and would become restless if too much time passed without the opportunity to participate actively. What I didn't realize then is that there are different ways of participating. To help everyone in my workshops learn, I had to discover how to recognize, understand, and respect the differences among my learners.

In Chapter 8, you learned about the different kinds of learning preferences. Those preferences affect the different ways in which people participate in the learning process. For example, people who learn well from listening and observing may speak up rarely, if at all, yet be as fully engaged as their colleagues. Those who process information quickly are likely to be the first to jump in with answers to questions, and those who like to take a little time to process might not at first seem to have an answer. People who like to jump right in and try to do something might seem more enthusiastic than those who like to think things through before taking action, yet the latter group might be just as involved and interested as the former. Your challenge as a trainer is to treat everyone as an individual, respecting everyone's differences and allowing people to participate in their own ways while making sure that they are engaged enough to learn.

Think About People's Experiences with and Expectations About Training

I sometimes imagine that when people walk into the door of a training room, they are dragging a suitcase filled with expectations: "This is going to be boring, boring, boring. I wonder what time we'll get a break." "He'd better not ask me to do anything stupid." "I hope we're going to have some fun." "I've can't wait to find out about this stuff." "If this gets embarrassing, I'm out the door."

People's experiences with training create expectations that affect their willingness to become engaged and their ability to learn. They might arrive expecting a difficult or uncomfortable experience because they've sat through too many lectures, been put on the spot too many times, been asked to participate in activities they found embarrassing, or spent too much workshop time playing games that were fun but had no point. They might have attended a workshop with a charismatic trainer whose personality helped the day fly by, even though they didn't learn much. They might expect the workshop to be one long game show, like the one they enjoyed so much a couple of months ago.

If part of your preparation was to elicit participants' concerns about training, you might already know a little about some people's experiences and expectations. The questions they ask when they come in the door or when the workshop starts may provide useful clues. I've found that the best way to deal with the negative or unrealistic expectations that may have resulted from previous experiences is to explain clearly right at the beginning what people can expect in *this* workshop and involve people right away in a relevant, non-threatening but engaging activity.

Check What You Know

List three actions you can take to encourage people to participate actively in a workshop.

1. _____

   _____

   _____

2. _____

   _____

   _____

3. _____

   _____

   _____

Strategies for Encouraging Participation

No matter why people attend training, how they differ in terms of the way they learn, and what baggage they bring with them, there are steps you can take to engage them and encourage them to participate actively.

- *Help them understand why they are learning.* Looking back, I completely understand why the participants I found so difficult in the mandatory incident report writing workshop were so resistant to participating. As far as they were concerned, the training was something that the powers that be had decided they needed. They had no say in the matter and no inkling of what the training could possibly do for them. Only by helping them understand the ways in which learning to write incident reports would help them do their jobs more quickly and easily did I have a chance of getting them engaged.

  It all goes back to the single most important question to address when it comes to engaging people in the learning process: "What's in it for me?" In other words, "What does this training have to do with me? What am I going to get out of it that's worth the time and effort of being here?" You can count on every participant having that question, even if he or she hasn't articulated it. Help people answer it, and you'll have gone a long way toward securing their participation.

- *Demonstrate respect for the participants' knowledge, skills, and experience.* Adults bring a great deal of knowledge, abilities, and experience into training. They know a lot more than you do about the work they do, for example. To gain their trust, let them know that you value and respect what they already know and are able to do. If you can increase their trust, you are also likely to increase their willingness to participate.

- *Establish an expectation for participation.* People are more likely to participate when they know that they will be expected to do so. You can start to establish that expectation when you make contact with participants before the workshop: Explain that this will be an interactive workshop, built around activities that will help them learn. During the opening, get people participating right away by using simple, relevant, non-threatening activities that encourage them to do something, speak to one another, and speak to the group.

Pay attention. From the moment that people come in the door, listen carefully to what they say and watch their body language. For example, a question like, "Will we have to do role plays?" probably means, "I hate role plays." A participant who sits slouching in the chair with her arms folded may be saying, "Just try to get me involved." Those clues help you identify issues or individuals who might need special attention.

Create a safe environment. Learning always entails some risk. Learning in a group means being willing to reveal a lack of knowledge, give up control, and make mistakes in front of other people. For people to take those risks, they need to feel that they will be supported, not judged. Make it clear at the outset that you encourage questions and differing points of view, you believe there are no "dumb" questions, and you think that mistakes are learning opportunities. Explain that you will be asking for volunteers for certain activities—such as role plays—but that everyone should feel free not to volunteer. Never put anyone down or respond with sarcasm to comments or questions, and make sure that all the participants treat each other with respect. When you or any of the participants give people feedback, focus on behavior, not on personalities. Recognize people for their efforts as well as their successes.

Use a seating configuration that encourages participation. In a traditional classroom setup, some people have the tendency to sit back and say, "Teach me." A seating arrangement in which people can see and hear one another easily and that encourages them to interact with one another as well as with the trainer is more likely to draw those people in.

Send Encouraging Messages

Body language, facial expressions, and encouraging words send messages that let people know that you want them to participate and value what they say. Some examples:

- Smile and make eye contact. Have you ever noticed the way an infant or small child responds when you meet his eye and smile? More often than not, he will smile in return. Smiles make us feel safe. Eye contact connects us to other people. Smiling and making eye contact with people in a workshop conveys the message that it's safe for them to be there and venture their opinions and ideas, that you are interested in them, and that you value what they say.
- Take a few steps toward the person who is speaking or about to speak. Moving in the person's direction conveys the message that you are interested in what the person is saying or about to say. Be careful, however, not to get too close, which could make the person uncomfortable.
- Nod and make noises of encouragement such as "uh huh," "good," "interesting," or "exactly right" at appropriate moments while a person is speaking or when he or she is finished.
- Say "thank you." Conveying appreciation for people's contributions sends the message that what they have to say is worthwhile, encouraging others to speak up: "That's a great idea, Margo. Thanks." "I really appreciate your bringing that issue up, Phil."
- Be sincere. People can tell immediately if there is a disconnect between what you say and what you feel. It's better not to say anything unless you can find something to appreciate in what a person has said.

Check What You Know

Which of the following statements describe effective ways of handling participants' questions?

1. _____ Prepare in advance by thinking about questions that people are likely to ask and deciding how you will respond.
2. _____ Try to respond as fully as possible to every question, even if it's beyond the scope of the workshop.
3. _____ Instead of answering every question yourself, turn some of them over to the group to answer.
4. _____ Repeat or paraphrase questions if you're not sure that everyone in the group has heard them.
5. _____ Bluff if necessary, so you can avoid compromising your credibility by saying that you don't know the answer to a question.

How to Respond to Questions

In a learner-centered workshop, trainers encourage participants to ask questions. Those question help participants engage with the content so they can learn. The questions also help the trainer discover how well people are learning, recognize what needs to be clarified, and find ways to focus the training more precisely on their needs and concerns. Here are some pointers:

- Prepare in advance by thinking about what questions participants are likely to ask and how you will answer them. Bring supplementary information available that you can refer to if someone asks a question you can't answer. If you are unable to answer a question, suggest where the person might find the answer or say that you'll do some research and get back to the person.

- Listen to the question carefully. Notice any body language or tone of voice that might suggest the person is really asking another question or wants to bring up another issue. If you're not sure what the question is, ask the person to clarify it before you respond.

- Before answering the question, repeat or paraphrase it unless you are certain that everyone in the group has heard and understood what the person asked.

- Don't feel as if you need to answer every question yourself. It's often very helpful to turn a question over to the group: "Does anyone know whether . . . ?" "Can anyone tell us how . . . ?"

- Avoid letting questions take the workshop off track. If someone asks a question that's beyond the scope of the workshop or raises an issue that you are not prepared to deal with at the moment, say, "That's an interesting question, Elliot. We don't have time to discuss that issue right now, but let's put it in the parking lot. We'll take another look at it later" or "We're going to talk about that topic this afternoon, Brenda. Please remind me if I don't get to that question."

- Be honest if you don't know the answer to a question. You will seldom, if ever, be an expert in the subject matter for the workshops you teach, and people are more than likely to ask at least a few questions that you can't answer. If you can't answer a question, say so, and if no one in the group has the answer, suggest where it might be found or offer to find it: "Miriam, that's a great question, and I don't know what the answer is. I'll see if I can find out and get back to everyone next week."

Tips for Collecting Questions

Questions are an important part of the learning process, but addressing off-topic questions can eat up valuable time. Also, some people are reluctant to voice questions in front of the group. I use the following techniques to collect questions in an organized way and encourage the less assertive participants to ask their questions.

- At the beginning of the workshop, ask people to write one to three questions they have on a piece of paper, fold the paper, and hand it in to you, signed or unsigned, as they prefer. Explain that you will be addressing most of the questions during the workshop, but you want to be sure that you address them all. You can also ask people to write down their questions right before or right after lunch. Save time at the end of the workshop to quickly address any questions that were not already answered.
- At the beginning of the workshop, ask participants to work in small groups to brainstorm the questions they'd like answered by the time they leave; write the questions on a flip-chart page, and post the page.
- Post a flip-chart page on which participants can write any questions that come up for them during a time when the group is doing something else.

4. How to Handle Behavior Challenges

Check What You Know

Which statements about handling behavior challenges are accurate?

1. _____ When addressing behavior challenges, it's important to focus on the behavior, not the person.
2. _____ It's best to wait to address offensive or hostile behavior until you can pull the person aside for a private chat.
3. _____ If someone continues to behave very badly, the best way to handle the situation might be to humiliate the person in front of the group.
4. _____ No matter how challenging someone's behavior, there is always a reason for it.

Every trainer has stories about participants whose behavior made them seriously consider getting into another line of work, one that didn't involve close contact with people: the production supervisor who paraded his superior knowledge in front of the group at every opportunity; the accountant who sat in the corner all day, checking e-mail on her phone; the customer service manager who called her colleagues "lazy and stupid"; the marketing associate who interrupted every three minutes with long, rambling questions; the computer specialist who wandered in half an hour late and slipped out several times during the day; the team that saw the workshop as a forum in which to voice complaints about management . . . the examples are endless.

It's not easy to know when and how to step in to address challenging behavior. If you step in too quickly or in the wrong way, you can offend, anger, or embarrass people. But if you let the behavior go on too long, other participants may become uncomfortable and the learning environment may be compromised. There are some strategies below for dealing with specific types of challenging behavior. First, here are some general guidelines and strategies to keep in mind:

- Help the group establish its own ground rules that deal with behavior and invoke them as needed. Examples include "listen while other people are talking"; "respect other people's points of view"; "no personal attacks"; "give others a chance to speak"; and so on.

- Use the parking lot for issues that people are concerned about but which are beyond the scope of the training or not immediately relevant. People might have trouble paying attention during the workshop because they are concerned about something else that's going on in the workplace. Acknowledging their issues and concerns might be all they need so that they can focus on the material covered in the workshop.

- Don't wait to deal with challenging behavior that is interrupting the workshop or making other participants uncomfortable. In particular, address offensive or hostile behavior immediately. You're in charge, and the participants expect you to be responsible for maintaining a positive environment.

- Focus on the behavior, not the person. How often have you heard people say, "She's too unpleasant to be around" or "He's the most annoying person I've ever met"? Trainers sometimes do that when they are talking about workshop participants they found difficult to deal with: "She was so thoughtless that she offended almost everyone" or "He was one of those arrogant, know-it-all types."

But what matters in a workshop isn't the participant's personality or personal characteristics—it's the way the participant behaves. Telling someone that she is being rude or arrogant is likely to offend or embarrass her—and it will do little to change the behavior. (She probably won't agree with you, anyway.) Instead, focus on what she is doing. Describe the behavior and explain the way in which it is interfering with the workshop. Say clearly what you want her to do differently: "Nina, several people were offended when you said. . . . I would appreciate it if you would not make any more remarks like that." "Peter, I can see that you know a lot about . . . , but I would appreciate it if you would give other people a chance to speak up during discussions."

- Always treat people with respect. No matter how badly a person behaves, never, ever attack or humiliate him, either in front of the group or when you speak to him privately. People always have reasons for their behavior. It doesn't matter to you what those reasons are; what matters is that you resist the temptation to judge, blame, or label the person, and that you treat him with respect. Sidestep arguments, and do not take challenges personally. If possible, talk to the person privately, during a break, or at the side of the room while others are working on an activity. If a participant's behavior is seriously disrupting the workshop, you might have to ask him to leave.

How to Deal with Common Behavior Challenges

Once you've been training for a while, you'll learn to discriminate between behavior that is simply annoying and behavior that is disruptive, and you will develop your own strategies for dealing with the different challenges. Here are some strategies that I and other trainers have found helpful for handling the most common challenges. You'll find lots of others sources for ideas in the Resources section at the back of this book.

People Who Talk too Much

Some people come to a workshop bubbling over with things to say. While they often make valuable contributions to the discussions, they may ramble and go on and on long after the point has been made.

It's important to realize that "talkers" may not realize how much they are talking. Try interrupting politely, recognizing the value of the contribution, and offering someone else a chance to speak: "Alicia, those are great ideas. Now let's hear what someone else has to say." If you have several "talkers" in the workshop, you can try to establish a time limit, but I've found that time limits can be difficult to enforce. If someone continues to go on and on, it can help to speak with her privately: "Alicia, you have some really great things to say, but I'm concerned that not everyone is getting a chance to speak in the time we have available. I hope you'll understand if I sometimes interrupt before you're finished or ask you to let someone else respond to a question."

People Who Dominate the Conversation

"Dominators" are similar to—and sometimes the same as—the people who talk too much. But dominators are more aggressive. They are always the first to jump in with an idea or an answer to a question. They may think that they know more than everyone else, feel a need to show everyone how much they know, or just like to be the center of attention. They tend to become impatient while others are speaking, and either interrupt the speaker or "rehearse" what they are going to say instead of listening.

It can be tricky to deal with dominators, especially those who want to show off what they know. You might say something like, "Jason, it's clear that you really know a lot about this subject, and I'd like to talk to you about it in more detail during the break. Now I'd like to get some of the other perspectives in the room."

Another strategy for keeping dominators in check is to establish a ground rule that after a person has spoken, he must wait until at least three other people have had a chance before speaking again. When troubled by dominators and excessive talkers, I sometimes ask that people raise their hands when they have something to say and then limit the number of times I call on the dominator or the excessive talker. It's not my favorite strategy because it smacks of the classroom, but it tends to work.

People Who Talk too Little

You already know that silence doesn't necessarily imply that someone is not interested and engaged. Some people speak only when they feel they have something important to say, and some are just very uncomfortable speaking up in a group. Be aware of silent participants' body language. You can tell when someone is alert and focused; the person is probably learning and it doesn't matter if she seldom speaks. You can often tell when a participant has something to say but is reluctant to jump right in and say it—she might be leaning slightly forward with an eager expression, perhaps glancing around the room—and you can offer her a chance to speak. Body language such as slumped shoulders and a refusal to make eye contact can also be clues that someone is feeling upset or angry. In those instances, you might want to speak privately to the person: "Allison, I notice that you're sitting back during the discussions. Is there something you'd like to say that you're not comfortable saying in the group?"

There are various non-threatening ways to encourage the more silent participants to speak. For example, you can ask them to respond to a question or discuss an issue with a partner or in teams of three instead of in front of the group, then ask for volunteers to share highlights of their team's discussion. You can gently nudge reluctant participants whose body language indicates that they have something to say by calling on them: "Bernie, did you have an idea about how we could . . . ?" But be sure not to push. If the person shakes her head, or says "No," just move on. And be sure to leave enough time for the person to think about his response; silent participants are often those who like to think things through before speaking.

One strategy to encourage silent people to speak up is to "poll" the group—"Let's go around the room and get one strategy from each of you." You can do the same thing by going around to the tables—"Let's get a couple of ideas from each table"—and then calling on individuals at that table. Offer participants a chance to pass so that they don't feel as if they have been put on the spot.

People Who Start Side Conversations

I hate it when the people behind me keep talking during a movie or a concert. That behavior is also annoying during a workshop. If possible, deal with it in a way that doesn't embarrass the talkers. As suggested earlier, you can try walking toward the people who are talking together, while continuing to address the group or focusing on the person who is speaking—that sometimes does the trick. You can establish a "no side conversations" ground rule at the beginning of the workshop and invoke it as needed. You can say something like: "Could we have just one conversation at a time, please?" or "Daniel and Rebecca, could you please hold that conversation for the break?" If a few people seem unable to resist side conversations, think of a reason to split them up: "For this activity, I'm going to ask you to work with people you haven't worked with before."

People Who Make Jokes to Gain Attention

Someone with a good sense of humor who is able to make people laugh from time to time can be a welcome addition to a workshop. But not all "class clowns" contribute to the learning environment, and not all people who make jokes are funny. In fact, these people can actually take control of the group, making it very difficult for you to keep things on track and manage the learning process. Let everyone enjoy humor that's appropriate and funny, but step in if it becomes disruptive. One way to do that is to give the person some attention by asking a question related to the topic under discussion: "Sasha, how would you handle . . . ?" "Marcus, what do you think would be the results of . . . ?"

Always step in immediately if an attention-seeking participant's comments are offensive or inappropriate, or if the person begins making fun of someone else, whether or not the object of the "humor" is in the workshop. Explain clearly that the comments or jokes are inappropriate, and ask the person to stop: "LuAnn, I'll have to ask you not to make those kinds of jokes or comments in this workshop." If the behavior continues, ask the person to leave.

People Who Are Negative and/or Hostile

Occasionally, you will have a workshop participant who is openly negative, argumentative, challenging, and even hostile. It doesn't happen often, but it does happen, and that kind of behavior poisons the learning environment.

When someone challenges you in that way, the first thing to do is take a deep breath and remain calm. Remember that it's not personal; the person is lashing out because of something that has nothing to do with you or even with the workshop. Be very careful not to let the participant draw you into an argument. Instead, let the person know that you acknowledge and respect his point of view, and, if possible, turn to someone else or the rest of the group: "Lars, I understand that you see this situation differently and that you have strong feelings about it. I wonder whether someone else has another point of view?" "Odette, I agree that what we're suggesting means making some big changes, and it will be difficult, but I'd really like to see whether we can think of some ways to make it work. [Turning to the group] How about the rest of you? What ideas do you have?"

If a participant continues to be openly negative or hostile, you'll need to talk to the person privately, and right away, even if you need to call a break or give everyone a quick activity so you can pull the difficult participant out of the room. Explain that you understand that she does not agree with what is being taught or would prefer not to be at the workshop, but that her comments and behavior are making it difficult for others to learn. Offer the person a chance to leave; if she decides to stay, insist that she participate in a more positive way.

Managing the Group in a Virtual Workshop

Virtual trainers face many of the same challenges when managing their group, including people who talk too much, silent participants, and people who are argumentative or make offensive comments. In some ways, the technology makes it easier to keep disruptive behavior from interfering with the learning process—you have much more control in a virtual workshop than when everyone is together in the same room. For example, you can ignore a raised hand icon if someone tries to dominate discussion or interrupt other participants. If necessary, you can go so far as to cut off the audio link if someone insists on starting arguments or making offensive comments.

Here are a few suggestions for avoiding and dealing with the challenges that might come up during a virtual workshop:

- When the workshop begins, explain the procedure by which you will call on people to speak and establish ground rules relating to such issues as time limits.

- Ask participants to use the chat function to bring up issues they are concerned about or would like you to address.

- If a participant is always the first to raise his or her hand when you ask a question or continues to leave the raised hand icon up while others are speaking, mention that you want to give everyone a chance to participate. If necessary, send the person a private chat message.

- If people are silent for too long, call on them by name—"Henry, would you like to chime in on this?" or send them a private chat message to make sure that the person hasn't left his computer.

Delivering Training Workshops: Pfeiffer Essential Guides to Training Basics.
Copyright © 2010 by John Wiley & Sons, Inc.
Reproduced by permission of Pfeiffer, an Imprint of Wiley. www.Pfeiffer.com

Quick Quiz

List the three to five key learning points from this chapter that will be most helpful to you.

_____

_____

_____

_____

_____

Apply What You Learn

What are some specific actions you will take to manage your learning group so that everyone is able to get the most out of the workshop?

_____

_____

_____

_____

_____

_____

What's Next?

You've nearly finished this book. You've learned how to plan, prepare for, open, and deliver a workshop. In the last chapter, you'll learn how to close a workshop in a way that helps participants use what they learned and how to evaluate the success of the training.

Answers to Exercises

Check What You Know

Here are some typical situations you might encounter in a workshop. Which strategy would be the best for handling each situation?

1. ___C___ One of the workshop participants keeps interrupting other people while they are talking.
   A. Say, "Andrea, you're talking too much. Please stop interrupting everyone."
   B. Ignore the behavior and be grateful for the person's energy and enthusiasm.
   C. Say, "I'd like to remind everyone that we established a ground rule about interrupting while others are talking. Let's try to honor that ground rule."

2. ___A___ A participant in the back of the room lounges in his chair, never makes eye contact with you, never responds to a question, and refuses to do the activities.
   A. Speak with the person privately during a break.
   B. Make it a point to call on the person by name.
   C. Ignore the behavior as long as he isn't bothering anyone.

3. ___B___ Two participants keep up a running dialogue with one another while you are speaking.
   A. Stop your presentation and ask, "Albert and Carla, why don't you tell us what's so interesting?"
   B. Continuing to speak, walk in the direction of the talkative participants and stand close to them until they stop talking.
   C. Ignore them for the moment and then call them aside during the next break.

4. ___B___ Participants are so enthusiastic that discussions are going on too long and veering into interesting directions that are not directly related to the subject of the workshop.
   A. If the discussions are productive, let them go on as long as people are interested, then drop an activity or two to make up for the lost time.
   B. At the beginning of the workshop, set up a parking lot for important issues that come up but are not related to the topic at hand.
   C. Stop every discussion when the time is up, no matter what.

Check What You Know

Which of the following statements would you agree with?

1. ___ When a workshop is mandatory, you can expect that most of the people who attend are likely to resist participating actively.
2. _X_ People can be participating actively even if they seldom speak up.
3. _X_ People's experiences with training can affect their willingness to become engaged and their ability to learn.

Check What You Know

Which of the following statements describe effective ways of handling participants' questions?

1. _X_ Prepare in advance by thinking about questions that people are likely to ask and deciding how you will respond.
2. ___ Try to respond as fully as possible to every question, even if it's beyond the scope of the workshop.
3. _X_ Instead of answering every question yourself, turn some of them over to the group to answer.
4. _X_ Repeat or paraphrase questions if you're not sure that everyone in the group has heard them.
5. ___ Bluff if necessary, so you can avoid compromising your credibility by saying that you don't know the answer to a question.

Delivering Training Workshops: Pfeiffer Essential Guides to Training Basics.
Copyright © 2010 by John Wiley & Sons, Inc.
Reproduced by permission of Pfeiffer, an Imprint of Wiley. www.Pfeiffer.com

Check What You Know

Which statements about handling behavior challenges are accurate?

1. _X_ When addressing behavior challenges, it's important to focus on the behavior, not the person.
2. ___ It's best to wait to address offensive or hostile behavior until you can pull the person aside for a private chat.
3. ___ If someone continues to behave very badly, the best way to handle the situation might be to humiliate the person in front of the group.
4. _X_ No matter how challenging someone's behavior, there is always a reason for it.

10

How to Close and Evaluate a Workshop

Check What You Know

Cybelle's workshop is almost over. She's pretty pleased with the way it's gone—Leon's suggestions helped her keep things moving, stay on track, and manage the group. But she has two more things to do: close the workshop in a way that helps people use what they've learned and evaluate the workshop to determine how well it met its goals.

   Leon gave her some advice for handling the closing and told her about the evaluation process. What are some of the things that he told her about how to close a workshop? About how to evaluate the success of the training?

_____

_____

_____

_____

_____

_____

I once attended an experimental theater production that had no ending. Two hours after the play began, the actors stopped what they were doing and walked off the stage. The house lights came up, illuminating a sea of faces with confused expressions. Was the play over? Was this just an intermission? Finally, one person stood up, and then another, and soon the entire audience was filing out of the theater, wondering what had happened and why the story was left up in the air.

In retrospect, I realized that the people who put on that play wanted us to be confused about whether to leave or not, and to feel unsure about how the story might have ended. That was the experiment. Although it was interesting, it wasn't an experience that I cared to repeat—it left me with an uncomfortable feeling and a suspicion that I had wasted my money. But it did provide an important insight about the importance of the closing to the success of a training program: Without an effective closing, people are liable to leave a workshop with a feeling of uncertainty about what they have learned and a suspicion that they might have wasted their time and money.

Here's what you'll learn in this chapter:

- Why a closing is important
- What a closing needs to accomplish
- How to evaluate a workshop

Many training programs run out of steam at the end. . . . How unfortunate! What happens at the end needs to be "unforgettable." You want participants to remember what they've learned. You also want participants to feel that what they learned has been special.

Mel Silberman, *Training the Active Way*

1. Why a Closing Is Important

Here are descriptions of the ways in which three trainers close their workshops. Which closing would be more useful?

1. _____ Marcus says, "Let's review what we've done today." He summarizes the key learning points, which he also shows on slides. He reminds participants about the importance of using what they learned once they are back on the job. He asks whether anyone has questions, but no one does, so he says, "Tomorrow morning you'll receive a link to an online evaluation, and I'd appreciate it if you'd fill it out right away." He pauses. "I guess that's it. Thank you for attending today, and good luck." He shuts down the projector and starts taking flip-chart pages off the wall while the participants gather up their things to leave.

2. _____ Lee gives participants three minutes to write down the key learning points from the workshop in their workbooks, goes around the room to elicit those learning points, and writes them on a flip-chart page. He then asks participants to work in pairs to come up with three actions they can take to apply what they have learned on the job and make a commitment by completing an action planning worksheet. When they have finished their action plans, he asks the group for ideas for learning more about the topic and writes them on a flip-chart page. Then he says, "You've done great work today. Please complete the online evaluation you'll receive tomorrow, and I encourage you to get in touch with me if you have questions while you apply what you've learned." As people gather up their things, he mingles among the group saying goodbye.

3. _____ Georgia says, "We're just about done. Does anyone have any questions before we leave?" Two people raise their hands while others start to gather up their things. One of the questions is about parking validation; the other is about an issue that came up earlier in the day. "I wish we had time to discuss that problem," Georgia says. "But we've already gone five minutes over. If you'd like to stick around, I'll be glad to talk to you about it." She turns off her microphone and begins disconnecting her laptop from the slide projector.

Delivering Training Workshops: Pfeiffer Essential Guides to Training Basics.
Copyright © 2010 by John Wiley & Sons, Inc.
Reproduced by permission of Pfeiffer, an Imprint of Wiley. www.Pfeiffer.com

The opening of a workshop gets people ready to learn; the closing should get them ready to use what they've learned when they are back on the job. Neglecting the closing because you've run out of time or don't realize its importance can leave people feeling that "So . . . that was interesting . . . now what?"

A useful closing is more than saying, "Thank you for your participation and please fill out the evaluation before you leave." The closing is an essential part of the learning process. The final activities of the workshop should help participants pull together the key learning points, recognize what they're achieved, and transfer the learning to the workplace by focusing on what they're going to do next. You might think of the closing as a bridge—people have spent some time on one side of the bridge collecting things they need; on their way to the other side, they will stop on the bridge to sort through what they have collected, decide what to keep and what to discard, and make plans about how to use the things that are important to them.

There are several important tasks to accomplish during the closing. Here are some of them:

- Review the key learning points.
- Address remaining questions and unresolved issues.
- Identify next steps.
- Make action plans and commitments.
- Recognize and celebrate success.
- Elicit participants' comments about the workshop.

Reviewing the Key Learning Points

In the short life-span of a workshop, people cover a lot of material and participate in a lot of activities. Before they leave the training room, you need to help them pull it all together. To save time, some trainers simply put all the key learning points on slides and read them off, but that doesn't do much to help participants think about what they have learned. It's much more helpful to lead a discussion or do an activity that encourages participants to come up with the key learning points themselves.

An easy, quick way to do that is to go around the room, elicit one or two learning points from each participant, and write them on a flip-chart page. But there are many other ways in which to accomplish that task. You'll find lots of ideas in books and articles on training. Here's a sampling:

- Ask participants to work individually, with partners, or in small groups to come up with a summary of the key points they would include in a short presentation for their colleagues or their managers about what they learned during the workshop. Ask volunteers to share the key points they came up with and write them on a flip-chart page.

- Ask participants to work in small groups to list the key learning points on flip-chart pages, post the pages, and then walk around the room and read the other groups' pages.

- Create a review in the form of a game, such as Trivial Pursuit, Concentration, or Jeopardy.

- Ask participants to work on their own, with partners, or in small groups to create job aids they can use after the workshop.

- Lead a brainstorming session to elicit advice, guidelines, ideas, or strategies that participants would give to colleagues who were not able to attend the workshop.

Addressing Questions and Dealing with Unresolved Issues

The closing is a time to wrap up all loose ends and shift the focus from the training session to the workplace.

Elaine, Biech, *Training for Dummies*

There are invariably a number of loose ends that need to be tied up at the end of a workshop, such as questions that have not yet been answered and issues that have not been addressed. You will seldom have time to deal with all of them, but leaving a few minutes in the agenda to deal with the most important will help provide people with a sense of closure.

Start with any items that remain in the parking lot. Go through the list quickly and cross out the ones that the group agrees are no longer relevant or no longer seem important. Then address any that you can address quickly, and enlist the group's help in deciding how to handle the remaining items. For example, a participant might volunteer to get information to clarify a policy or research an issue related to team responsibilities.

Once you've dealt with the parking lot, ask whether participants have any remaining questions and try to answer them in the available time. Keep your eye on the clock—there will still be some important things to do before people leave. If people raise relevant questions that cannot be answered quickly, record them on a flip-chart page and offer to get back to them after the workshop.

Helping Participants Identify Next Steps

For a workshop to result in change, participants need to leave with ideas for how they can use and build what they have learned. One way to help them come up with ideas is to lead a brainstorming session. Ask such questions as,

"When you're back at work, what steps can you take to apply what you've learned?" and "How can you continue to learn more about . . . ?" Write all the ideas people come up with on a flip-chart page and ask people to select the ones that will work best for them.

You can make this a small-group activity in which participants brainstorm their ideas in small groups and then share what they come up with in the large group. You can also turn the activity into a gallery walk—post flip-chart pages around the room and ask participants to write their ideas on the pages. When the pages are full, give participants a few minutes to walk around, read the pages, and record ideas that they like in their workbooks. This activity has the advantage of getting people up and on their feet toward the end of the workshop when they might be feeling restless.

At the conclusion of any program that has featured active training, participants will naturally ask, "Now what?" The success of active training is really measured by how that question is answered, that is, how what has been learned in the class affects what participants will do in the future."

Mel Silberman, *Training the Active Way*

Check What You Know

Which of the following statements about action planning are true?

1. _____ An action plan can be used in place of a test because it serves essentially the same function.
2. _____ The larger the scope of an action plan, the more useful it will be.
3. _____ People are more likely to carry out the commitments on their action plans when they have shared those commitments with someone else.
4. _____ An action plan is more useful when it includes a deadline.

Helping Participants Make Action Plans and Commitments

The value of a training workshop is determined by what people *do* with what they have learned. But there is a big difference between thinking, "This is great stuff—I'm going to use it every day" and "During the next six weeks, I will schedule time to meet at least once a week with each person on my team to talk about his or her work." People are far more likely to apply the learning if they have developed written action plans and made public commitments to taking those actions.

A useful action plan is specific, not vague. It describes concrete steps and includes a realistic deadline. It is also limited in scope. People who try to change too much at one time are likely to become frustrated and stop trying. It's far more effective to focus on one or two actions at a time: "join Toastmasters"; "use a checklist to plan my next meeting"; "ask open-ended questions during hiring interviews"; "teach the seven-step problem-solving process to my team"; "make expectations clear the next time I delegate a job."

Just as the action plan should include concrete steps, it should specify when the actions will be taken: "for the next two weeks"; "by the end of March"; "within the next three months"; "the next time I. . . ." If appropriate, it should also specify what resources and assistance the person needs to take the action and where he or she will get them.

Remind participants that the action plans they do at the end of the workshop are just a starting place. Action planning is an ongoing process—when people have accomplished what they set out to do, they should do a new action plan, again focusing on one or two key actions with specific deadlines.

The last part of the action planning process is to make a public commitment. People are more likely to do what they say they are going to do when they have told someone else that they are going to do it. You can give participants a few minutes to explain their action plans to one another, even to give a signed copy to a partner. You could ask them to write "commitment memos" to colleagues or their managers. You could also ask them to write memos to themselves and give them to you so you can send them back in a few weeks.

At the end of the chapter, you'll find an action planning worksheet that you can adapt for the workshops you deliver.

Check What You Know

What's the purpose of saving time at the end of a workshop to recognize and celebrate participants' accomplishments? What are some ways of doing that?

_____

_____

_____

_____

_____

_____

Celebrating Participants' Accomplishments

By the end of a workshop, participants have worked hard and achieved a lot. An activity that helps people celebrate their hard work and success closes the workshop on an upbeat note and encourages them to continue learning. Ideas for a celebratory activity range from asking for volunteers to mention something they appreciated about their colleagues during the workshop to having a party.

As a trainer, I always take a moment to thank the participants and acknowledge the work they've put in and what they've accomplished. I make my comments as specific as possible: "I appreciated your

Ways to Recognize and Celebrate Success

- Do a brief activity in which participants say what they appreciated about working with one another.
- Ask participants to write down one thing they accomplished on flip-chart pages posted on the wall and to read what everyone else wrote.
- Hand out certificates and/or rewards.
- Have a party, with food and party favors.

Delivering Training Workshops: Pfeiffer Essential Guides to Training Basics.
Copyright © 2010 by John Wiley & Sons, Inc.
Reproduced by permission of Pfeiffer, an Imprint of Wiley. www.Pfeiffer.com

willingness to tackle thorny issues"; "I appreciated the way that you respected your colleagues' points of view, even when they differed from yours"; "The way that you jumped right into the activities, even when they were difficult or felt uncomfortable, was great!"

2. Evaluating the Workshop

Check What You Know

1. What are the reasons for evaluating the success of a workshop?

   _____

   _____

2. What are some ways in which to gather information for an evaluation?

   _____

   _____

3. What are some of the questions to ask during an evaluation?

   _____

   _____

   _____

   _____

Workshop evaluations provide valuable information about what's working well and what might need to be changed the next time the same or a similar workshop is delivered. Evaluations can be as simple as asking participants a few questions about how well the workshop met their needs and expectations to as complex as calculating the organization's return on its investment.

There are different methodologies for evaluating the success of a training program, but most of them are based on the work of Donald L. Kirkpatrick, who describes four questions that evaluations are intended to answer.

1. *How satisfied were participants?* This question is usually asked at the end of a workshop or immediately after it is over. The purpose is to learn how well participants thought the workshop meet their needs, how well they thought the trainer did, whether the content seemed complete and useful, how well the activities helped them learn, whether anything seemed to be missing or unnecessary, and so on.

   This type of evaluation is the most common, because it is the easiest to use. Some trainers leave a few minutes at the end of the workshop to ask participants, "What worked today?" and "What would you change?" Many hand out a simple questionnaire they ask people to complete before they leave. Others send participants a link to an online survey right after the workshop, although it can be difficult to get responses from everyone once they have left the training room.

   The information provided by this type of evaluation needs to be considered carefully, because it is very subjective. Participants who like the trainer are likely to rate the entire workshop a success, and some who are not satisfied may hesitate to assign low ratings because they don't want to hurt the trainer's feelings. Conversely, a participant who really disliked one activity or component of the workshop might give the entire workshop a negative rating.

2. *What did participants learn?* This question might be asked at the end of a program, or it might be asked after some time has passed. The purpose is to discover the extent to which people gained new knowledge or skills or changed their attitudes. The information can be gathered by using a written or performance test or through observation, surveys, and/or interviews.

   Determining what people learned requires a baseline against which to measure the extent of the learning. For example, you can compare the results of a test or survey given to participants before the workshop to the same test or survey given to them after the workshop, or you can use a performance checklist to assess their performance both before and after training. But it's important to remember that knowing how to do something or being able to give correct answers to questions on a test does not necessarily mean that someone can and will actually apply the learning.

Delivering Training Workshops: Pfeiffer Essential Guides to Training Basics.
Copyright © 2010 by John Wiley & Sons, Inc.
Reproduced by permission of Pfeiffer, an Imprint of Wiley. www.Pfeiffer.com

3. *To what extent have participants changed their behavior as a result of training?* Because the overall goal of a training program is to change behavior or performance, this is the most important question to ask. But it is also a question that can be very difficult to answer; for that reason, relatively few training programs receive this level of evaluation. For one thing, the question cannot be answered until people have had an opportunity to apply what they learn. There needs to be a baseline against which to measure changes, and it can be difficult to separate the effects of training from other factors. For example, a manager might not have had a chance to use what she learned about conducting hiring interviews because there has been a hiring freeze or there is no data available against which to compare a participant's post-workshop ability to give performance feedback with his behavior before training.

4. *What were the results of training?* This method evaluates how well the training achieved the desired outcome. Although this is a very important question, training programs are rarely evaluated at this level because it is difficult to do, requires information that is not usually readily available, and requires special expertise on the part of the people doing the evaluation.

There is a related question that is being increasingly asked of training programs: Was the program worth the cost? Evaluating the return on investment, or ROI, of training requires a great deal of information and expertise. For more, see the work of author and researcher Jack Phillips.

Closing and Evaluating Virtual Workshops

There isn't much difference between closing and evaluating a virtual workshop and accomplishing those tasks for a live, in-person workshop. Consider these points:

- When you develop the script, block out time for a closing, especially a key learning point review and action planning.
- Send the link to any evaluation form or survey you will be using immediately after the workshop. Tell participants that it's coming and ask them to complete it right away.
- Tell participants what to do if they have questions after the workshop is over.
- Thank participants before signing off.

Quick Quiz

List the three to five key learning points from this chapter that will be most helpful to you.

_____

_____

_____

_____

_____

What's Next?

You've reached the final chapter of this book. Now it's up to you to build on what you have learned and use it to deliver successful training workshops. There's an action planning worksheet on page 240 to help you get started.

Apply What You Learn

1. List the key learning points that you would like participants to take away from your workshop.

   _____

   _____

   _____

   _____

2. Design an action planning worksheet for your workshop on a separate sheet of paper or on your computer.

3. List steps participants could take to follow up the workshop.

   _____

   _____

4. Describe the way in which you will help participants celebrate success.

   _____

   _____

5. Decide what you will do to evaluate the workshop and describe what you will need for each level of evaluation you plan to use.

   ❏ Ask participants to complete a questionnaire to rate their satisfaction with the workshop.

   _____

   _____

   ❏ Use a test, survey, interviews, or observation to measure what participants learned.

   _____

   _____

   (Continued)

❏ Use observations, data, surveys, and/or interviews to measure the extent to which participants changed their behavior as a result of training.

_____

_____

❏ Use data, surveys, and/or interviews to assess how well the training achieved the desired outcome.

_____

_____

❏ Use data to evaluate the return on investment and determine whether the training was worth the cost.

_____

_____

Answers to Exercises

Check What You Know

Here are descriptions of the ways in which three trainers close their workshops. Which closing would be more useful?

1. ___ Marcus says, "Let's review what we've done today." He summarizes the key learning points, which he also shows on slides. He reminds participants about the importance of using what they learned once they are back on the job. He asks whether anyone has questions, but no one does, so he says, "Tomorrow morning you'll receive a link to an online evaluation, and I'd appreciate it if you'd fill it out right away." He pauses. "I guess that's it. Thank you for attending today, and good luck." He shuts down the projector and starts taking flip-chart pages off the wall while the participants gather up their things to leave.

2. _X_ Lee gives participants three minutes to write down the key learning points from the workshop in their workbooks, goes around the room to elicit those learning points, and writes them on a flip-chart page. He then asks participants to work in pairs to come up with three actions they can take to apply what they have learned on the job and make a commitment by completing an action planning worksheet. When they have finished their action plans, he asks the group for ideas for learning more about the topic and writes them on a flip-chart page. Then he says, "You've done great work today. Please complete the online evaluation you'll receive tomorrow, and I encourage you to get in touch with me if you have questions while you apply what you've learned." As people gather up their things, he mingles among the group saying goodbye.

3. ___ Georgia says, "We're just about done. Does anyone have any questions before we leave?" Two people raise their hands while others start to gather up their things. One of the questions is about parking validation; the other is about an issue that came up earlier in the day. "I wish we had time to discuss that problem," Georgia says. "But we've already gone five minutes over. If you'd like to stick around, I'll be glad to talk to you about it." She turns off her microphone and begins disconnecting her laptop from the slide projector.

Delivering Training Workshops: Pfeiffer Essential Guides to Training Basics.
Copyright © 2010 by John Wiley & Sons, Inc.
Reproduced by permission of Pfeiffer, an Imprint of Wiley. www.Pfeiffer.com

Check What You Know

Which of the following statements about action planning are true?

1. ___ An action plan can be used in place of a test because it serves essentially the same function.
2. ___ The larger the scope of an action plan, the more useful it will be.
3. _X_ People are more likely to carry out the commitments on their action plan when they have shared those commitments with someone else.
4. _X_ An action plan is more useful when it includes a deadline.

Action Planning

Date:

Topic: *Delivering Training Workshops*

1. When you started reading this book, you thought about the objectives you would like to accomplish. Turn back to the Introduction and review those objectives. Then look at the key learning points you wrote at the end of each chapter.

2. Describe two or three specific actions you will take to use what you have learned to deliver successful workshops. Include the time by which you will take each action (by end of quarter; within thirty or sixty days; by September 1). Indicate what resources you will need and where you will find them. When you have accomplished these actions, make a new action plan.

Action	Time	Resources
1.		
2.		
3.		

Resources

The publications, websites, and associations on this list are only a few of the excellent resources available for learning more about training. You can find books that are out of print at Amazon.com and other online booksellers. Also check out www.HRDPress.com, www.AMACOM.com, and www.Pfeiffer.com for other great training resources.

Publications

Allen, Michael. *Michael Allen's 2009 e-Learning Annual*. San Francisco: Pfeiffer, 2009.

ASTD. *2007 State of the Industry Report*. Alexandria, VA: Author. (www.astd.org)

ASTD. *2004 Competency Model*. Alexandria, VA: Author. (www.astd.org)

Barbazette, Jean. *The Art of Great Training Delivery: Strategies, Tools, and Tactics*. San Francisco: Pfeiffer, 2006.

Biech, Elaine (Ed.). *90 World-Class Activities by 90 World-Class Trainers*. San Francisco: Pfeiffer, 2007.

Biech, Elaine. *Training for Dummies*. Hoboken, NJ: John Wiley & Sons, 2005.

Bloom, Benjamin S. *Taxonomy of Educational Objectives*. Boston: Allyn and Bacon, 1984.

Bowman, Sharon L. *Training from the Back of the Room!: 65 Ways to Step Aside and Let Them Learn*. San Francisco: Pfeiffer, 2008.

Caffarella, Rosemary S. *Planning Programs for Adult Learners* (2nd ed.). San Francisco: Jossey-Bass, 2002.

Clark, Ruth Colvin, and Kwinn, Ann. *The New Virtual Classroom: Evidence-Based Guidelines for Synchronous e-Learning*. San Francisco: Pfeiffer, 2007.

Clark, Ruth Colvin, and Mayer, Richard E. *e-Learning and the Science of Instruction* (2nd ed.). San Francisco: Pfeiffer, 2008.

Conley, Chip. *PEAK: How Great Companies Get Their Mojo from Maslow*. San Francisco: Jossey-Bass, 2007.

Covey, Stephen R. *7 Habits of Highly Effective People*. New York: Simon and Schuster, 2004.

Diamond, Robert M. *Designing and Assessing Courses and Curricula*. San Francisco: Jossey-Bass, 1998.

Fee, Kenneth. *Delivering e-Learning: A Complete Strategy for Design, Application and Assessment.* London: Kogan-Page, 2009.

Foshay, Wellesley; Silver, Kenneth; and Stelnicki, Michael. *Writing Training Materials That Work: How to Train Anyone to Do Anything.* San Francisco: Pfeiffer, 2003.

Gardner, Howard. *Multiple Intelligences: New Horizons in Theory and Practice.* New York: Basic Books, 2006.

Gargiulo, Terrence L. *Once Upon a Time: Using Story-Based Activities to Develop Breakthrough Communication Skills.* San Francisco, Pfeiffer, 2007.

Gargiulo, Terrence L., Pangarkar, Ajay M., and Teresa Kirkwood. *The Trainer's Portable Mentor.* San Francisco: Pfeiffer, 2008.

Goad, Tom W. *The First-Time Trainer. New York:* AMACOM, 1997.

Goman, Carol Kinsey. *The Nonverbal Advantage: Secrets and Science of Body Language at Work.* San Francisco: Berrett-Koehler, 2008.

Gronstedt, Anders. Training in Virtual Worlds: Training Technology and e-Learning. *Infoline, 25.* Alexandria, VA: ASTD, 2008.

Gupta, Kavita. *A Practical Guide to Needs Assessment* (2nd ed.). San Francisco: Pfeiffer, 2007.

Hodell, Chuck. *ISD from the Ground Up: A No-Nonsense Approach to Instructional Design* (2nd ed.). Alexandria, VA: ASTD, 2006.

Kirkpatrick, Donald L., and Kirkpatrick, James D. *Evaluating Training Programs: The Four Levels* (3rd ed.). San Francisco: Berrett-Koehler, 2006.

Knowles, Malcolm S., Holton III, Elwood F., and Swanson, Richard A. *The Adult Learner: The Definitive Classic in Adult Education and Human Resource Development* (6th ed.). Amsterdam: Elsevier, 2005.

Kolb, David A. *Experiential Learning: Experience as the Source of Learning and Development.* Upper Saddle River, NJ: Prentice-Hall, 1984.

Lawson, Karen. *The Trainer's Handbook* (2nd ed.). San Francisco: Pfeiffer, 2006 (updated edition, 2008).

Leatherman, Dick. *Training Trilogy: Conducting Needs Assessment, Designing Programs, Training Skills* (3rd ed.). Amherst, MA: HRD Press, 2007.

Leigh, David. *The Group Trainer's Handbook: Designing and Delivering Training for Groups* (3rd ed.). London: Kogan-Page, 2006.

Mager, Robert F. *Preparing Instructional Objectives* (2nd ed.). Belmont, CA: David Lake Publishers, 1984.

Nadler, Leonard. *The Handbook of Human Resource Development.* Hoboken, NJ: John Wiley & Sons, 1984.

Pike, Robert W. *Creative Training Techniques Handbook: Tips, Tactics, and How-To's for Delivering Effective Training* (3rd ed.). Amherst, MA: HRD Press, 2003.

Silberman, Mel. *Training the Active Way*. San Francisco: Pfeiffer, 2006.

Society for Human Resource Management (SHRM). *2006 Workplace Forecast*. Alexandria, VA: Author. (www.shrm.org)

Stolovitch, Harold D., and Keeps, Erica J. *Telling Ain't Training*. Alexandria, VA: ASTD, 2002.

Thiagarajan, Sivasailam. *Thiagi's Interactive Lectures*. Alexandria, VA: ASTD, 2005.

Thorne, Kaye, and Mackey, David. *Everything You Ever Needed to Know About Training* (4th ed.). London: Kogan Page, 2007.

Weimer, Maryellen. *Learner-Centered Teaching*. San Francisco: Jossey-Bass, 2002.

Wilder, Claudyne. *Point, Click & Wow!: The Techniques and Habits of Successful Presenters* (3rd ed.). San Francisco: Pfeiffer, 2008.

Magazines, Websites, and Newsletters

Websites and the addresses of web publications change frequently. If you are unable to find a magazine, website, or newsletter using the web address on this list, try a web search for an updated address.

Accelerated Learning Network Newsletter: www.accelerated-learning.net

ASTD Learning Circuits articles: www.astd.org/lc

Creative Training Techniques Newsletter: www.creativetrainingtech.com

Don Clark/Big Dog, Little Dog: nwlink.com/~donclark, bdld.blogspot.com/

eLearn Magazine: www.elearnmag.org

Ignite Newsletter: www.kenblanchard.com/Business_Leadership/ Management_Leadership_Newsletter/

www.intulogy.com/library

Learning at Light Speed weblog: www.learningatlightspeed.com

Performance Improvement Journal (PIJ): www.ispi.org (resource center)

Peter Honey and Alan Mumford's Learning Styles Questionnaire, www .peterhoney.com

www.roiinstitute.net

Training and Development: www.astd.org/TD/

Training magazine, Lakewood Publishers: www.trainingmag.com

Associations and Organizations

These associations and organizations are excellent resources for people in the training field, offering information, learning opportunities, publications, blogs, conferences, networking, and more.

American Society for Training and Development (ASTD), www.astd.org/

American Management Association (AMA), www.amanet.org

The e-Learning Guild, www.elearningguild.com

International Association of Facilitators (IAF), www.iaf-world.org

International Society for Performance Improvement (ISPI), www.ispi.org

Society for Human Resource Management (SHRM), www.shrm.org

About the Author

Janis Fisher Chan, a writer, editor, instructional designer, and trainer, has been in the training field for more than twenty-five years. As a co-founder of Write It Well (formerly Advanced Communication Designs), a training company that specializes in helping people communicate clearly and work together productively, she designed and conducted a wide range of training programs on topics that ranged from business writing to negotiating and consulted with clients on training-related issues. She is the author of *E-Mail: A Write It Well Guide—How to Write and Manage E-Mail in the Workplace* and other books in the Write It Well series; Pfeiffer's *An Academic Manager's Guide to Meetings*; and the American Management Association's self-study courses *How to Manage Your Priorities* (2nd ed.); *Delegating for Business Success; Presentation Success*; and *Communication Skills for Managers* (5th ed.). She also served as an instructional writer and developmental editor for the highly acclaimed *Leadership Challenge Workshop, The Five Dysfunctions of a Team* Workshop Kit, and other books and training packages for Pfeiffer and other publishers. After receiving her master's degree in theater from San Francisco State University, she returned to the university to complete a post-graduate program in organization development. She lives in Marin County, California.

Index

rules, 131, 200, 214, 215–216; establishing rapport, trust, and credibility, 112, 126–127; helping people get to know you and one another, 123–124; icebreakers, 125; parking lot "page" to keep things on track, 132; Plan Your Opening Worksheet, 138; providing logistical information, 132; providing preview of workshop, 130; setting the stage with, 121–123; stimulating interest and engagement in learning, 124–125; virtual workshop, 132–134

"Out-the-door" reminders, 199

P

Pagers, 131

Parking lot "page," 132

Participant preparation: gaining managers' support as part of, 61–63; importance of, 47–48; pre-work assignments to, 55–58; selection of participants, 4–5, 49–55; for virtual workshops, 59–60

Participants: accessibility to special needs, 29; answering workshop concerns by, 130; attendance motivation by, 203–204; body language of, 207; demonstrating respect for, 206; encouraging discussion participation by, 202–208; gathering information on, 8; greeting and making them feel welcome, 118–120; handling difficult, 194, 211–217; helping them learn, 169–190; making action plans, 229, 238–240; making eye contact with, 144, 147, 149; using name tents vs. tags for, 127; notifying, 4–5, 51–53; opening activities to engage, 121–134; pre-workshop contact with, 8; preparing the, 5; providing logistical information to, 132; putting them at ease, 113; responding to questions by, 209–210, 220; seating arrangements for, 23–25, 32–38; sending e-mail reminders to, 55, 120; training expectations and experiences of, 204–205; "welcome" e-mail to, 54; what to do before arrival of, 113–117; what to do when they arrive early, 119; WIIFM (What's in It for Me) and, 53, 129–130. *See also* Audience; Managing learning groups

Personal appearance, 91, 97–98

Personal preparation primer, 89–91

Phillips' ROI evaluation, 234

Pike, B., 51, 70

Plan the Learning Environment Worksheet, 45–46

Plan Your Opening Worksheet, 138

Planning: action, 229–230, 238–240; backup or contingency, 6, 82; closing and evaluating workshops, 223–237; learning environment, 4, 22–40, 41; opening activities, 120, 121–134; Plan the Learning Environment Worksheet, 45–46; Plan Your Opening Worksheet, 138; scheduling workshop, 4, 13–22. *See also* Meeting planning workshop

PowerPoint slides: practicing with your, 101; tips for using, 158. *See also* Slide projectors

Practicing your delivery, 99–102

Pre-work assignments, 55–58

Preparation: for getting started with workshop, 109–138; importance of, 2–3; issues to consider during, 7–8; materials, 5, 69–86, 116; of participants for learning, 4–5, 47–68; self-preparation by trainers, 5–6, 87–107; supplies, 5, 39, 69–86, 116; tasks of, 3–6. *See also* Checklists

Preparation Checklist Worksheet, 9, 12

Privacy issues, 28

Pronunciation, 154–155

Props, 101

Q

Questions: allowing everyone a chance to answer, 180; closed-ended and open-ended, 189; guidelines for best use of, 176–180; learning role of, 174–175; making lectures interactive, 175; managing workshop, 209; responding to, 209–210, 220; tips for collecting, 211. *See also* Discussions

Quick Quiz icon: closing and evaluating workshops, 235; getting started, 134; helping people learn, 187; managing learning groups, 218; preparing materials and supplies, 83; preparing participants to learn, 63; scheduling/ planning learning environment, 40;

CPSIA information can be obtained
at www.ICGtesting.com
Printed in the USA
BVHW060627130619
550896BV00013B/163/P